ISRAEL

ACRE
HAIFA

JENIN

NABLUS
TEL AVIV
JAFFA
RAMALLAH

LYDDA
RAMLE

JERUSALEM   JERICHO

ISDUD
BETHLEHEM

MAJDAL

GAZA   Dead
HEBRON   Sea

BEERSHEBA

KHALASA
ASLUJ

AUJA

River Jordan

S·R

IRAN
(PERSIA)

IRAQ

D0934714

ISRAEL
REVISITED

ISRAEL
REVISITED

by Ralph McGill

WITH A FOREWORD BY BILLY ROSE

TUPPER AND LOVE, INC., Atlanta

Publishers

Appreciation is expressed to The Atlanta Constitution *and to the Overseas News Agency for permission to use much of the material in this book.*

Printed in the United States of America

FOOTE & DAVIES, INC. • ATLANTA

To my Mother

*and to the memory of my Father and
my Grandmother who have already
crossed over Jordan*

Foreword

Eඅඋඅඒ IN 1949, my missus and I took a trip around the world, and one of the countries we got to see was Israel. At the time, many of the streets of Tel Aviv, Haifa and Jerusalem were still criss-crossed with barbed wire, and the roads leading through the hills of Judea were littered with burned-out trucks. Nevertheless, thanks to an old Chevvy and a pair of even older legs, I managed to see most of this tiny country, and when I left it a few weeks later I was pretty excited about what I had seen.

When we got back to New York, my old boss, Bernard M. Baruch, asked me to put my enthusiasm in my pocket and try to estimate Israel's chances of survival in this highly competitive world. I told him that one swing around the globe wasn't enough to make an economic expert out of a Broadway jumping-jack, but that I had come away from Israel with the general impression that its people were (a) intelligent, (b) tough as nails, and (c) prepared to work like all get-out to make a go of their new lives.

"A business or a nation with those qualities usually gives a good account of itself," said Mr. Baruch.

Since my visit, I've heard nothing to change my snap appraisal of Israel's chances. On the other hand, I've read darned little on the subject which could be classed as good objective reporting. Most of the favorable stuff was too favorable—obviously the work of men who were out to make as good a case for the new nation as possible. And as for the dissenters—well, as was to be expected, most of them sounded as if they were carrying a 2,000-year-old chip on their shoulders.

Last week the galleys of Ralph McGill's book on Israel showed up on my desk and I began to thumb through them out of a sense of duty. But what started as duty quickly became compulsion, for McGill, editor of one of the South's most trustworthy papers, *The Atlanta Constitution,* had obviously gone to Israel with an open mind and crammed it with facts and figures before making it up.

I've met Ralph once or twice, and before I was halfway through his book I found myself wondering how this soft-spoken and hard-headed gentleman from Georgia had come to write such an incisive and insightful commentary on the complicated events now shaping up at the far end of the Mediterranean.

I got to thinking about it and, as I hunch it, the answer is triple-pronged: First, McGill is an Irishman, which means that while he has a lively sense of justice in general he has no axiom to grind about Israel in particular. Second, he is first, foremost and fastidiously a newspaperman, avaricious for facts but plenty leary of special-pleading propaganda. And third, he has a long record as a fighting Southern liberal, and once he's gotten his facts straight he's not one to by-pass those touchy areas where even angels fear to tiptoe.

When I finished reading "Israel Revisited," I was, of course, tickled to find that McGill's conclusions jibed with mine, but that's neither here nor there. The important thing is that, without pulling any punches, he has written a book about this controversial little country which one can read without prejudice or without suspecting the author of same.

Here, at last, is a meticulous and meaningful answer to the often-asked question, "What's Israel really like?"

New York   —BILLY ROSE
August 30th, 1950

Contents

1

"And Winds Austere and Pure"

Israel now, and Palestine before,
were many things to me. Two lines from Stevenson express well
one of my impressions:
> *"Hills of sheep, and the homes of the silent*
> *vanished races,*
> *And winds austere and pure."*

There were many meanings. It was to me Assyrian bowmen
and their bows twanging in the fields of Armageddon; the Persians, the glint of sun and sea on armor; at Acre the sound of
Crusader trumpets and cavalry charges and engines before be-
seiged cities. It was Moses on Nebo and Joshua and the old
Prophets, and Christ and the politicians and the clergy in Jerusalem plotting to pull Him down.

When I went there first, I came away with a feeling of having
lived with great plans; of having been in currents strong and
deep; and also of having dwelt for a time in the Leatherstocking
Tales in modern dress, as actors sometimes have done with *The
Taming of the Shrew.* I felt, too, although I was too self-
conscious to say so at the time, a sort of spiritual refurbishing
from what I had seen and experienced. When I went back in
the spring of 1950 to see in Israel the nation restored to life after
2,000 years, and witnessed every human and social problem being
met with a mixture of mystic exaltation, sweaty toil and realism, I
felt it once more. I was not unaware of the flaws, the failures, and
the jarring contradictions, but I came away feeling as if I had left
old friends with whom, in some distant past, I had worked and
played and hoped. And I came away feeling stronger, younger
and surer about the eternal verities and the dignity of man.

As a boy, I came up in the country and in the Presbyterian

faith, and if the hot breath of Calvin has not always been strong upon my neck, it is no fault of my family. I grew up knowing the old hymns in which Jordan's "Stormy banks," Galilee, and "Jerusalem the Golden" were sung mightily on the Sabbath and at Prayer Meetings. As a boy I used to dream of some day seeing the golden domes of Jerusalem and the blue reaches of the Sea of Galilee.

My grandmother, who was a "Blue Stocking" Presbyterian, was responsible for this. She yearned all her years to see the Holy Land. In her last years, she would walk out on the front porch of our farm house in East Tennessee, which looked across a meadow and a bottom field where Indian corn grew every year, to the Tennessee River and say, reflectively, "Son, we've all got one more river to cross . . . the river of Jordan." I did not know, being then but a young boy immensely fond of his grandmother, that she was speaking symbolically. I used to ponder on it and wonder why all of us Presbyterians someday would have to cross over Jordan. At any rate, the pull of the ancient land there on the Mediterranean was planted in me as a child.

In 1938, I spent some time in Europe. In Germany I looked and read and talked. In February of that year, I saw Hitler parade to the Kroll Opera House across from the burned ruins of the Reichstag Building, and then went in to hear him speak. I made plans then to go on to Austria. I felt what was coming. I saw the Nazis in Vienna and it was not pretty. In that city I had, even, a few very minor cloak-and-dagger experiences visiting Jews whose friends in America had given me their names and addresses. I brought out some valuables for one of these. Those wretched days of witnessing shameful human degradation stirred me deeply. When the Austrian plebiscite of April 10, 1938, was over, I departed. I have been wrong a lot of times, but later on, from England, I wrote that if Czechoslovakia fell it meant war for us all.

I came out of Austria convinced, too, that the idea of a Jewish homeland in Palestine was one which had to be translated into fact. This was long before the gas chambers and the crematoriums. I had seen relatively little violence, really, in 1938—men forced to scrub sidewalks while jeering crowds stood by laughing;

property taken. But witnessing human beings reduced and destroyed by the constant pressure of fear and uncertainty was enough to convince me then of the necessity for Palestine. Had someone then suggested the Ringstrasse led on to the concentration camps and their incredible horrors, I would not have believed it. That hideous development was in the Nazi bloodstream, but we had not the proper microscopes for discovering it.

It was the war, the journeys to Europe during it, and after the guns had stopped, when I saw the camps and the Nuernberg trials, that made me know I had to go to Palestine.

So, in 1946, I went. In 1950, I went back to see the nation of Israel. The "goy" who went in 1946 was no Zionist. I went utterly unprepared for what I saw. Looking back on the experience when I was in Paris enroute home, I knew for sure I had met people to whom I felt drawn. I knew, too, I had somehow been allowed to see inside their dream and to experience the almost tangible vitality and spirit of it. I came away feeling as if some years had slipped away from me. I felt spiritually uplifted. It seemed to me I had touched there on the frontier farms, in the small holder cooperatives and in the spirit of the people, the realness of the brotherhood of man. I never tried to rationalize what I had seen in terms of politics, although I was, of course, aware of the gigantic struggle in that field. It was the people and the great unity and spirit of sacrifice and determination that touched me. I am sure it was the same spirit that was present in the days when our own country was being founded. One feels it in the Declaration of Independence, in the preamble, and in the amendments to the Constitution. The spirit of the times comes through the words. When I came away from Palestine, I was sure that if fighting came, there would be a very real and desperate resistance. I never asked to see leaders of the Haganah or of one of the terrorist underground groups. I sensed their strength and will.

So, I was not greatly surprised when war did come and the Israeli army came out of the ground and fought well enough to win a victory. The whole story of that war, small as it was when compared with the great ones, will be difficult to tell. There are chapters about young men who went into battle but a few days after their arrival on immigrant ships and helped hold Jerusalem. They appear and disappear into the dust of the ancient land across which they marched. There are individual acts of heroism and madness which are lost in the developing folklore.

The Kibutzim (farms) played their part well. They had been strategically located, if not always economically. They were the frontier outposts about which, before which, and over which the flood of war poured. Some changed hands often. Others held out from their machine gun positions and slit trenches. A few were overrun, their dead buried yet in the ruins.

I had been confident since 1946 the people would fight well. I was fearful only about the well-trained Arab Legion of Transjordan. One could count on the Egyptians to do about what they did—to bog down because of poor leadership and lack of any general will to die for their king. As it turned out, the Arab Legion was all that saved an Arab rout. And while there is no love lost, there is mutual respect between the Israeli and Legion soldiers.

When I returned to Israel in the spring of 1950, I saw the battle lines, the ruins, the villages and the roads where men fought and died to hold the land that comprises the nation. I went back to the farms of the previous visit and saw again the industry expanding but still inadequate.

Again I experienced the lift of spirit and the feeling of being drawn to these people building a country. It is too bad, or at least I think it is too bad, that some have tried to picture the people as almost mystic heroes and heroines dwelling on some distant and magic Olympus. There has been too much romance about Israel in one direction and not enough in another.

Of course, they have their fools and fanatics. And naturally they have political shysters along with their intelligent, sacrificing, magnificent leaders. They have a few loafers who came thinking it was all dream and no work. It is not perfection.

The religious problem is a difficult one, with conflicting sects of orthodoxy. They compose a political bloc which long will have to be reckoned with and appeased by compromise until the passing of time makes evident to all the Talmud must, in part at least, be reinterpreted in the light of the 20th century, and its technology. (The Moslems have already done so with the Koran.) At least, that is how it seemed to a Presbyterian-reared "goy." The religious story is absorbingly human. It also is, and was, inevitable.

There are a few in Israel, of course, who are extreme nationalists and who argue furiously that all Jews, especially American Jews, should come there. I recall a very unhappy European young woman in Jerusalem who was almost screaming that the Americans had bought a homeland "damned cheap." That there should be some like this is not startling, nor does it represent the Israeli opinion. Many Europeans fail to understand America. That a very few Israeli should so believe is natural. They have no way of knowing the meaning of America and cannot understand that in America Jews helped make the Revolution, were in the struggle for liberty, and have since been assisting in building America. Not all Americans understand that, even. So, I attached no more importance to extreme, untenable views in Israel than anywhere else. There are, too, the extremists in the Mapai party, who talk like the present Prime Minister of Romania or Bulgaria. But the people know them and the leading party, Mapai, exposes them successfully.

The real story is the great dream coming true and the men and women who are sweating and working to make it so, the people who keep coming—the Yemenites lifted by the long arms of aviation from the Middle Ages; the Iraquians brought from the dark alleys of that ancient land; the Jews from North Africa— the poor, hopeful ones, coming with a few pots and a bundle of clothes.

The immigrant camps are a story. They cause the serious lag. There is not enough money nor skills nor housing to allow the newcomers to be moved out on schedule. And always more come.

But the glory of it is on every hand. I saw two men not long out of an immigrant camp working in a cement brick plant. The tattooed numbers of a Nazi prison were on their arms. Under the hideous numbers, the muscles moved smoothly. The alchemy of work and the chance to build a new nation had healed the wound of the meaning of those numbers.

And, of course, there are jealousies. The North African Jews think the Yemenites are being favored. The Yemenites believe the Middle Europeans get all the best of it. And so it goes. The camps are not pleasant places, and idleness breeds worry and moods. But once the camps are behind and there is a house and land, most of the brooding doubts evaporate. And certainly now and then there are one or two who want to go back or to go somewhere else. But they are few and their counterparts are in every great movement. They are not important, although they supplied the doubters and the Arab propagandists with material for the stories of an "underground railway in reverse." All these things are in the mixture. But they were never the story.

I was never without a sense of Bible history and story on either visit to the Holy Land. When, in 1946, I made my first sentimental journey from Nazareth to Bethlehem, to the Sea of Galilee and to the source of the Jordan River, I tried to picture the dust and the noises along the trail as the tribes set out from Nazareth to be taxed in Bethlehem, with others joining them in the Valley of Jesreel along the Plains of Armageddon. I felt the spiritual impact of the Sea of Galilee and the stalls below the old Crusader Church at Bethlehem. From Scopus and the old city of Jerusalem I looked toward the Dead Sea and remembered the old Prophets and the patient Nazarene. There were soldiers and there was strife there in His time, and the records of armies and soldiers are written from the Via Maris to the other end of the land.

I remembered it all again when I went back in the spring of 1950.

It is something of all this I have tried to tell in the chapters ahead—of that visit in 1946 and of the Israel born of the birth pains of those years.

2

To Palestine Via the Nuernberg Trials

Nuernberg, Germany (1946)—On the way to Palestine the only logical route seemed to go to Paris, take the night military train to Frankfurt, a jeep to Nuernberg, and a bus to the square, dark old courthouse of the shattered town.

Mechanically, the trials of the German war criminals are perfect. The lights are bright. The electron's miracle makes it possible to put on earphones and listen in any of four languages at the same time a witness or attorney talks in one.

There are quick translations neatly mimeographed. The refurnished courtroom is warm and comfortable no matter how wretched and cold it may be outside, regardless of how grim and uncomfortable its dark, stone wings may be.

But all the while, sitting there listening to horror and cruelty piled on horror; all the time one's eyes watch on the screen the crawling, convulsive movements of a pile of dying bodies; all the while one sees the dead stacked high like so much grotesque cordwood, there is a growing impatience within one.

It does not go away if you stare at the prisoners, using field glasses to bring their second-rate faces up so close they seem to be staring right into your own eyes. You look them over carefully, 22 men in a dock.

"How in God's name," your mind asks, "did this ordinary bunch ever rise so high they threatened the world?"

You cannot answer it.

You look at Goering's porcine face with its pair of shrewd, greedy eyes; at Hess' strained countenance with its careful mask which might not be known as a mask were it not for his disappearance now and then to have his nerve-strain stomach ulcers treated. You look at stolid Schacht, at dapper von Ribbentrop. You feel the impatience rise again as they and their companions fret their last minutes on the stage.

You hear a voice in your mind saying that they do not really matter; that their punishment is of interest but for the moment and for history; that what they did is done and that what matters most is what is left to be done. You feel that the real trial is not there in the brightly lit, comfortable room and the earphones which will tell you the story in your choice of four languages.

This feeling will not go away when the witnesses are on the stand and you tune in to listen, your eyes wandering from the prisoner's dock to the witness and back again.

In all the testimony one fact stood out above all the others.

"By corruption, by denunciation, by terror, by debasing prisoners they sought to make human beasts of them . . . the system employed by the SS was to lower human beings to the lowest . . . to dehumanize them . . . always that before death . . . of life."

Day after day the witnesses came and went.

Horror, agony and terror rolled into the ears until they drowned the senses. Death seemed to be trying death. What was done was done. Nothing in the room, no decision or judgment, could undo it. The really important trial was somewhere outside. And you felt driven to find it. The trail leads to the "DP," or Displaced Persons, camps.

Before you see them—the persons and the camps—it is very easy to speak of them as DPs and DP camps. But not after you have seen them.

They are down in Bavaria. They are around Nuernberg. They are along the winding way from that city to Frankfurt. They are not far from Heidelberg. Even the battered city of Hanau has a camp on its outskirts. Polish trains coming into Berlin almost every night bring more persons for the DP camps, and every night there are a few who unfortunately died and for whom the final listing is DP—dead persons.

"What about the DPs?" you ask.

The answers are varied.

"Trouble-makers . . . poor devils . . . in the black market . . . idle and in trouble . . . agitators . . . Communists."

That, too, is before you have seen them.

Before you have seen them they seem to fit into generalities; the two letters are enough for conversation.

"The DPs are a headache . . . The Jews want to go to Palestine . . . It is an organized campaign . . . many Jews don't want to go . . . the Poles hate the Russians . . . the Baltic DPs won't go back unless they go back to independent countries . . . I hear some Jews want to leave Palestine . . . They are too insistent . . . The DPs are in the black market up to their ears." . . . DPs—DPs—DPs—the letters roll easily from the lips.

But the people? And the facts?

The first DP I saw, just by chance, was a girl. She had come to ask to see a doctor. On her arm was tattooed in blue ink an initial and a number. She had been at the Auschwitz concentration camp.

She had another tattoo mark. It was just at the base of her neck—in front where the collar bones meet at the breastbone. I had to ask what it was. They told me.

It marked her as having been "prostitute for officers only."

It meant that the day she arrived at the concentration camp they had taken her, along with others, and sent her to the houses where the officers went for pleasure.

I saw others like her. One was dancing for a camp show. She danced well. But I cannot forget her eyes. I was to see others in Palestine, on the collective farms.

It was impossible to ask. I suppose the ugly horror of that degradation is always in the mind. But if a little bit of it has dimmed I did not want to bring it back again. So I could not ask what was in their minds, how they had felt, how they felt now, what it had done to the pattern of their lives.

I saw an old man on the road. He had an old coat clutched to his side. He was going to trade it in the black market. There are others like him. Those who see in him something to criticize apparently never see the almost daily stories of American, British and Russian officers and men caught and convicted of large black market corruption. The old man with his coat was not important. His eyes, which were dead, and his face were weary from what they had seen and felt. I would not have liked to pull back the curtain from his memory. Or from others like him in the many camps where they wait for civilization to make up its mind. Old and young—they wait. And the waiting is long.

There is no generalization to be made about DP camps, except this one—there they are. There are the DP camps and there are the DPs. They are people. They must go somewhere.

No two camps are alike, yet all are the same. This trite, neat paradox grows out of the fact that all of them are housed in old barracks, some of them being old concentration camps redone. Others are housed in German buildings, some of which were spared the bombs, some of which have been repaired.

Some have staffs which are genuinely interested, sympathetic, intelligent and at work. These camps are easy to recognize. The faces in them look different. The organization of schools, crafts, recreation and the food gives evidence of interest and intelligence. In others the staffs don't know how to take hold, don't really care, have allowed their own inadequacy to make them sullen and resentful against their DPs—be they Jews, Balts, Poles or Ukranians.

They are all alike in that the people are alike and their problem is the same. Perhaps 30 percent of the displaced persons will go back to their native lands. When the chaos of postwar months lessens, some of the Poles, the Balts and Ukranians will go back to their old homes. I think, too, a very small percentage of Jews among the DPs will "go back." I think a few from Hungary will chance it. A few from Holland will try again. Some will go back to France. And to other countries which once were home.

But not many. Of 750,000 in Europe, at least 600,000 will never "go back."

The Jews learned something from this war, as did peoples in the underground in all countries occupied by the Germans.

But everywhere the lesson was plain to the Jews. Europe became a vast burial ground not merely because a Nazi party sought to make it so. An approximate 6,000,000 Jews died or were killed by executions, starvations or brutalities in Europe.

Jews whose families had been integrated in the life of Holland for 500 years were shocked to see Dutch brutality and hate come to the surface in a country they had never thought of in any other way but as their home and their country. It was the same, too, in Belgium and in France and in Norway. In Vienna, in Prague, in all the cities of Europe, were Jews whose families had been assimilated into the life and culture of those cities for centuries and who long ago had ceased to think of themselves as anything but nationals of their respective countries.

Out of that great shock has come a bitter and strong suspicion. It is something you have to see and feel, so tangible is it, in the DP camps of Germany, in the offices of men in France and even in faraway Egypt, which was untouched by gun or bomb.

I went to Europe for the fourth time during the war period believing that it was best an effort be made to repatriate the Jews, to enable them to go back to their countries and again become a part of the life of those countries. I publicly had expressed such an opinion in numerous editorials and columns of comment. I was entirely sincere.

It is with equal sincerity that I write I was wrong. Persons who are not survivors, or who have not seen these survivors, cannot know how haunted by the past are these people; how unbearable life would be if these people were forced to go back to live, among the graves of their people, awaiting God knows what. The DPs know, too, that in the scramble for property and the spoils left by the ousting of the Nazis, anti-Semitic actions loom large. The German sickness remains in the shattered cities and in the minds of Europeans like mustard gas in old shell holes, cellars and forests after a battle has ended.

That is why in France, Jews who had held high positions as Frenchmen and who would hold high positions again; who had opposed Zionism as a movement which might detract from the citizenship and successful integration of Jews elsewhere, sadly shook their heads and told the Anglo-American Committee of Inquiry they now believed immigration to Palestine necessary for the Jews of Europe. They, too, had seen and had changed their minds. It is not merely the old who want a place to finish out their years in peace; the middle-aged who want a place to "belong," it also is the young and militant Jews who are willing to die for such a place.

It is not too trite a paraphrase to say that if there were not a Palestine it would be necessary to invent one.

3

The Arabs Rattle the Saber

CAIRO, Egypt (1946)—In Egypt you talk with Arabs. That is not difficult. The contrary is true. They seek you out. They are charming and they are good hosts.

Having been in Egypt in 1945 during the formation of the Arab League, having heard personally from King Farouk his ideas on the future of Arab nationalism, which he leads and dreams of taking to high places, it was not difficult to pick up the threads a year later.

There are many forces at work, now as always, in the Middle East. But none is more interesting in its potential for evil or good than that of Arab nationalism. In considering it, it is necessary to look at the past.

The eighteenth century was drawing to a close before any influence of the Western world touched the Arabic lands. From the sixteenth century the Turks had kept the Arab peoples in a cultural status which made the previous dark ages of Europe seem bright in comparison.

It was Napoleon and the five-year occupation by the French, who brought an Arabic printing press, which kindled a spark. Syria was the second Near-Eastern nation to receive Western culture. Most of this came from American schools, more than a hundred of them being established in the old Syria, which included Lebanon, Palestine and Transjordan. The American University in Beirut is 75 years old and its graduates occupy many high places. These, with the French schools, brought an ability to read and write their own language; taught them some of the glories of their ancient past, and without doubt provided the stimuli for a cultural awakening.

An Arab nationalism was born. It came almost entirely from

Christian Lebanese educated in American schools. Naturally it had international tolerance, freedom from foreign restraints, religious and racial liberty as part of its creed.

It began bravely. But it soon was divided, corrupted and disregarded except for those parts of it which seemed to fit the various aspirations of "nationalism."

Firstly, it denied the chief tradition of Islam, which recognizes no nationality. The world is divided in two. In one part dwell the Moslems in the "Abode of Peace." In the other dwell all others in the "Abode of War." Islam is declared to be the only nationality worthy of a Moslem.

There were compromises. Egypt allowed religious freedom, but made Islam the religion of the state. So did Iraq. There are many Christians in Syria, so that nation ruled its president must be a Moslem. Only Lebanon, with its Christian majority, guaranteed full freedom of religious belief and practice. That small country and its Christian majority trembles today and it may come before the UNO asking for protection against the revival of Islam.

It was inevitable the broad basis of the original nationalism should fall apart. This was encouraged and assisted by the rival mandatory powers of France and Britain. Seeking to maintain their spheres of influence in the years between the two wars, it was necessary to resort to frequent uses of force. Failure to keep promises made to the Arab rulers during the World War I and the inability to govern without force, contributed to the destruction of any remaining moral force the powers might have had.

France's failure to keep the Free French promise made by their delegates, Gen. Georges Catroux, in 1941; and Britain's failure to keep the Balfour promise for Palestine and her efforts to carry water on both shoulders with regard to that question, have lowered these nations' moral prestige and power.

The result is that even the Arab League, which assuredly had the British blessing, is interested primarily in the Arab states and peoples. It has no love or even respect, for French or British.

It has this fatal weakness—there are wide differences and varying levels in culture and economic levels. The Arabs with the best culture and the most intelligent outlook on world problems are, by general consent, those of the Lebanon. The Arabs with the best standard of living are those in Palestine, with Lebanon perhaps second. It is almost impossible to describe how miserable and wretched is the lot of the average Arab. He is the most exploited of all peoples anywhere; he is illiterate to the degree that thousands cannot understand even their own national radio programs put on by their rulers and politicians who follow dynastic rivalries and retain old suspicions. The most accusing fact is that it is his own ruling class which has degraded and reduced him to so low an estate.

Perhaps the greatest strain, creating the most instability in the Arab seeking for a pan-Arab solidarity, is the growing gulf between the younger, modern-educated leadership and the antiquated, corrupt, feudal leadership which has held on for centuries. The former, without guns and possessed merely of an articulateness, was able to be the final straw which brought about the fall of the Egyptian government in February, 1946, and which sent the old tiger, Ismail Sidky Pasha, in as Premier with orders to cover his claws with velvet and placate the students with promises and kind words.

The tension is between a slowly developing white collar professional class and the feudal, immensely rich and powerful landowning class. As usual, the religious leaders are with this latter group and what is preached in the mosques is what they want preached.

The patient masses, diseased, hungry, miserable and ruthlessly and continually exploited, have not yet begun to stir. They are seeing that prices are higher; that food is less, but that some seem always to have plenty. The immutable laws of their religion which teach acceptance of one's status as the will of Allah, have not yet been broken down even in the cities as they have in India's great urban centers. But already some of the old line politicians are talking about reform.

There is another factor. Yesterday it was a cloud in the sky, hardly larger than a man's hand. Today it is at least as large as a sheepskin hung up to dry. Tomorrow it will be, I think, as large as a Bedouin's tent and then, one day, it will mushroom and the storm will break.

Pan-Islamism is growing. There are educated demagogues who have sickened of Farouk and Ibn Saud and the Arab League. In Cairo I was told by men who know that already the political leaders are troubled by it and do not know how to meet it.

Having made Islam their state religion they cannot oppose these fanatics who have started rolling up the snowball of the Pan-Islamic movement.

The movement is reactionary. It is right out of the medieval era in concept and plans for execution. It frankly is hostile to everything Western, especially to the Christian West.

All through the Middle East there is beginning to be smelt the smoke of this new "holy" and fanatical religious campaign. It was no idle public opinion expressed by Lebanese leaders in February that they might be forced to ask of UNO a sort of national home, similar to that being sought by the Zionists in Palestine, to protect the Christian peoples in the Lebanon and the Middle East. Pan-Islam is basically hostile to the Christian West. Its ideal is the ideal of Mahomet—to convert all the world to its faith. Its immediate objective is to unite all Moslems under the banner of the Prophet—and not in any Arab League.

It is growing because it appeals to the masses, whose instincts, like those of all masses everywhere, are crude and to the point. If it should be successful, it would endanger all Western institutions in the Middle East. Should the nations of the world fail to find in the UNO a working pattern for peace, Russia could take this one simple ideal and, by promoting it, obliterate even the most superficial aspects of Western culture and institutions.

It is against this confused, divided, changing background that one must consider Arabic opposition to the plan to open Palestine to Jewish immigration. The Arabs based their opposition largely on the fact they have been there for many hundreds of years. They insist the culture of Palestine is Arabic. They also ask why they should be removed. As I was to learn later on, both contentions are weakened by error. Yet, I think, aside from the cynically corrupt feudal landed class and the theologians, those who express these sentiments likely are sincere. The facts are, as one may learn by going to see, that the culture of Palestine rapidly is changing and the Arabs would not find it necessary to leave.

Nor can the Arab insist he was on the side of the democratic forces in the recent war or in the present struggle for democratic stability.

In the first and second world wars, the Germans sought to win over the Middle East, historic bridge between Europe, Asia and Africa. In both, they had some help. In the second war, both Syria and Iraq had to be occupied to prevent their rulers from handing them over to the Germans. Arab assistance helped the Germans early to establish landing fields in Syria for the use of bombers. In Palestine, the Arabs' Grand Mufti fled to the Germans. Egypt and the others, believing Germany would win, remained unhappily neutral.

All made fortunes out of the war, national and personal. Egypt possessed something like one billion dollars in sterling and dollar balances in London and New York when the war ended. They gained permanent installations worth hundreds of millions. Our railroad building in Iran, for instance, is an example.

In the greatest of all wars, Arab sympathies generally were with the Nazis and the Japanese. They overshadowed the exceptions.

You have these thoughts in mind when you book a ticket on the MISR (Egyptian National) Air Line for Jerusalem.

4

There Are Jewish Farmers

Jerusalem (1946)—Riding the 40 miles from Lydda airport into Jerusalem, I again arrayed in my mind what ideas I had about the Zionist movement and its relation to Palestine.

Again it was my conclusion that in America the Zionist story and proposals were a little too flawlessly and easily put; that the Arabs, even if one discounted their claims, were being pushed around too strongly; and that it would be a disappointment if it turned out that the program was built on money and emotional politics. There had formed in my mind an idea I would find a vast philanthropy; a horde of newcomers living off a dole. For many years I had believed Palestine ought to be opened for Jewish immigration, but, in my reading and interviewing, these other ideas had developed.

I had made up my mind that I would go to the Jewish Agency, ask for certain statistics to be prepared and documented, and then request to be shown what had been done and what was being done.

A chill, raw rain was falling and before we arrived at Jerusalem it had turned to a hard and driving hail which rattled off the windshield and made the old steel top sound as if a thousand woodpeckers had attacked it in a frenzy. So, we saw Jerusalem, glorious on her hills, through a curtain of pelting hail and mist which gave to her spires and minarets the color and shading of unreality, as if she were some castle-in-the-air.

But the hail did something else, too. It set me to thinking about the thousands of persons in the DP camps. I had seen some of them in snow and rain and cold. They had been disturbing my thinking for a long time.

The next day I was on the road. I had no special credentials, I had given no notice of my coming, nor had anyone else. At the Jewish Agency, by dint of asking, I had found Harry Beilen and Harry Levin, executives respectively of the Jewish Agency and the Jewish National Fund. They arranged for me to see what I wanted to see. That changed from day to day, often on the spur of the moment. It was not possible for any advance notice to be made of my arrival.

We started near Jerusalem, going first to Ma'Aleh Hahamisha, which is called in English, "The Height of the Five." It is named for five men who were ambushed and killed there by Arabs in 1937.

It is on a hill. The earth was still sticky and gumbo-like from the hail and rain of the day before. There were 720 dunams of land, a dunam being one-quarter of an acre.

But I wanted to see people and their work. I saw it.

The place was muddy. It was not prepossessing. The buildings were sound. There were a few walks. There was evidence of a tremendous amount of work having been done on the soil of that rocky hill.

It was a farm. It looked like one. It smelled like one. The persons who came and went about me were, for the most part, young. They were farm workers. They looked it, and, yes, they smelled like it. Their hands were hard with work; their faces and bodies were without fat, but strong and healthy-looking. I walked over the place. There were many fruit trees. They told me there were 100 acres of them, cherries, plums, apples and so on. There were 20 acres of vegetables and they told me of their business of selling seed and plants from their fruit tree nursery. They showed me the beginning of their forest. I saw their fields of pyrethrum, sold to makers of insect killers.

This was on a hill. The hills of Palestine are not easy to describe, except by poets. They can speak of their beauty and harshness of line; of the great rocky ledges which line each hill in terraces like so many blue-white ribs. In my Southern states in America, I have seen small farmers break their backs on poor, eroded land. Not one I know would tackle a hill near Jerusalem. Those hills make up two-thirds of all Palestine's land.

But the soil is not bad. I, who know a little about soils, could see that. There simply was not too much of it in any one place. Various earnest young men and one girl, with the gift of English, talked to me of the diverse soil structures, the preponderance of lime in some sections; of the rate of evaporation which was greater than the rate of condensation. They assured me the soil structure was deeper than it seemed. They often had a meter (40 inches) of top soil, they said, and they proved it.

There were 100 members of the community, men and women, 70 children of their own and 30 refugee children. Most of them, the original settlers and refugees, were from Poland and Romania.

The original settlers had come in 1934, a small nucleus to which had been added more in 1938. They had been wrestling with that hill ever since. They were winning. I could see that from the fields they had wrested from it and put into productivity. They were winning, but the hill still was a tough opponent. They had put trees on his back where none were; they had fields growing on him, between his huge ribs. He was fighting back.

We had lunch there. We ate in the community dining room. They came in, their shoes muddy, their clothes showing evidences of hard work and of having endured rain, hail and many hot suns. There was no hired labor. There never is any.

I looked at the hands at my table as they reached for and passed dishes. They were hard and used to work. We had cooked pumpkin, macaroni, good dark bread, margarine and a hot soup as the final dish. They finished and went back to work.

Everyone was a Jew. They, save for the refugees, had been winning that wrestling match with the hill across a span of 12 years. And they still had some wrestling to do before they pinned that hill. A swift recollection of some of the people I knew who often asserted Jews would not work with their hands came and went as swiftly. I was with persons who were alive, and doing things. The drama of it began to come to me.

Leaving, I saw the concrete block houses they had used years before, like our own frontier, pioneer forts, with slits for rifles. Now they are storage houses.

They looked at me questioningly.

"How about one that's further along?"

We drove into one which, as soon as we were within the gate, looked like a garden. There was no one about save some children playing.

"This place," they said, "is called Kiriath Anavim," which means "City of Grapes."

We found one kindly looking man, past middle-age, in the small room where the mail boxes were. His name was Chaim Mosel and he was the bookkeeper. He was resting after an illness.

Kiriath Anavim was like a garden. The farm was 26 years old. The settlement had pinned the shoulders of its mountain to the mat, had made a valley flourish, was surrounded by a tall forest of fine green trees, climbing thickly across and along the hill beyond.

It was a scene not to be forgot. Where their land ended, the garden ended. The sharp-lined, rocky hills stretched as far as I could see, ending in the horizon's haze. On them was no sign of life, man or plant.

Bookkeeper Mosel talked no English. Harry Levin translated for me as I asked my questions. The story ran thusly:

"We came in 1920, 30 of us at first, from Russia. Some of us had had training at the agricultural college in Odessa. Later there came a group from Poland and then a pre-Hitler group from Germany. Lately some refugees have come from Romania. There are 110 members, exclusive of our children, but the total on the farm is 300. There are 30 from Romania who are in training for farm work, going to work in the morning and school in the afternoon. We give courses in hill culture, dairying and horticulture.

"Some of our own children now are adult members."

I broke in to ask if any one had ever left this place.

"None," he said.

"The oldest child of the colony was in the English ATS (similar to our WAC) and her husband was in the Army. They are back here now and have their own child.

"Of our 110 adult members 14 served in the British Army."

The chief crops were apples, plums, peaches, grapes, milk and eggs. All the products were sold through the co-operative, called TNUVA.

There were 150 head of cattle on the farm. The average milk yield was 5,000 liters with some cows producing as much as 8,000 liters. They had found the Dutch breed did better than others.

They had 3,000 white leghorns and were increasing the flock to 4,000. I saw their chickens and equipment. It was all United States manufactured.

They had 1,800 dunams, of which 500 were in cultivation, the rest being in forest. Near Tel Aviv, they had 75 dunams on which they grew feed and carried on a sizable number of bee colonies.

I have never seen any farm anywhere with finer trees, flowers and grass, neater, cleaner barns and stables; a better poultry section. The farm was bringing in a substantial profit and had been for many years. It was, without any reservation, a magnificent farm.

I asked about the Arabs. It was obvious that this richly producing, well-kept farm was not bothered.

"We get along," he said. "Yesterday we had an Arab visitor from Ramleh. He told us he had seen in the papers where the Egyptians were demonstrating against the British. 'I wish the day might come,' he said, 'when we, too, might be rid of them and settle our differences.' We have been here a long time. Today we have had several of them visit our community Chairman, who is ill. Some are afraid to come because of the landlords. They come to our funerals, we go to theirs. They come to our doctor and dentist and there is no charge."

I asked about swapping farm knowledge. He smiled.

"We learned something from them," he said, through Harry Levin. "We improved on, but kept, the Arab system of terracing and hill plowing. But we have taught them machinery, new crops and methods."

There was no single idler about the place. Everyone was at work. They hired no labor, even though they were successful and established. They had spent a quarter of a century there and were started on the second. Their children were fitting in naturally as farmers, school-trained and accepting the life as their own. They knew no other. There were grandchildren of the original settlers coming along.

They had started as had the young men and women at "The Height of the Five." Their hill, too, had been barren and harsh.

Going out from its cool green gardens and trees, seeing its fields and vineyards, its barns and stables; hearing the sound of the poultry, I knew on that first day this was no mere program of money and emotions. Here was sweat and toil as hard as that done by any pioneers in any country. I had thought perhaps the colonies had been put down on well-bought, well-prepared land, with houses ready and tractors and tools waiting.

That first day I knew this was not true. Both had started with tents. Each had got a loan, paid interest, bought tools as they could and accomplished what they had by muscle and long hours of toil.

Going out, we came into the road between the barren hills, leaving the green fields behind where the fence ended. It was like another world, and it was. It was the ancient world that had been trampled by armies and conquest until it was worn and dying.

5

I Meet a Great Man

REHOVOTH, Palestine (1946)—We took the road north through the Judean hills. On them were the traces of ancient terraces. They had lasted for some centuries after the Turkish conquerors. But the Arab shepherd and his flocks, the unmended washes, the rain and wind were too much for them.

I was curious about the farms. The acreage was relatively small. I had seen what the farms of Denmark could do in a study of that country before the war. Palestine farms, once they were established, seemed to do even better.

At the Agricultural Research Institute, which is near the Sieff Scientific Research Institute, both being near Rehovoth, south of Tel Aviv, there was an answer.

It was had from Dr. I. Volcani, head of the Research Institute.

"Six good acres here," he said, "are equal to 25 in Denmark or Holland. We have a longer growing season and can get from two and a half to three crops a year from good land."

I was to meet many fine persons on the trip, in high and modest places. Dr. Volcani was one of the really great ones. It was he who had seen, more than a decade before, that Palestine's Zionist farmers could not go along on a hit or miss plan. They would have small farms. Therefore, an intensive small farm plan had to be developed. He set out to do it. He had splendid assistance. One of the things I was to find made plain day after day was that when civilization for a time was put down in Europe, Palestine began to get, and was continuing to get, not merely men and women passionately willing to toil and struggle without complaint, but men and women with great technical and scientific skills.

There were many heartbreaks and many failures in the early

days of Palestine. In the early years of the 19th Century many colonies failed. They had no plan. They came without guidance. They tried olives, almonds, various crops.

In 1909 experiments were begun. More than 20 years ago Dr. Volcani began new experiments. In 1927 he revised all his assumptions.

In 1928 on a series of farms he began a methodical recording of every act. This went on for six years. On irrigated and non-irrigated lands, of various soil types, the work went on. He tried new crops, new systems.

By 1930 he had 20 new crops for Palestine farms. He was getting four tons of cow peas off each dunam, that is off each quarter of an acre. He was getting 10 tons of millet or maize off a quarter-acre; four tons of green forage, four to six tons of sun flowers. Each crop was removed in three to four months. He was getting three crops per year to attain these figures. But he was getting them.

He spent 10 patient years documenting, checking, testing the system of crop rotation.

This, plus his years of checking his farm families to record all their work, food requirements, listing every egg, every chicken, every bit of food produced, bought, consumed, canned or preserved, meant he had spent 18 years to work out a plan or formula. In all the recorded history of agriculture no one man has done as much as he to give a country a crop plan.

But when he was done, he had something which made it possible for the Jewish Agency to say, backed by facts and deeds, that they could absorb many times more farmers, without displacing a single Arab, than the British experts said was possible.

The Volcani figures were as exciting as a fast-moving novel. You may see the records of 5,200 dunams of land in one colony which had been tested through the years. (Divide it by four to get the acres.)

In 1911, there were 10 farm families on that acreage. By 1918, he had 26 families on the same land and they were all living better than had the 10 original families. By 1938, he had 90 families on it and in 1945 there were 144 farm families on the same acres engaged in direct agriculture with 63 other families on it not directly in agriculture, they being blacksmiths, teachers, office workers and so on.

In the early years, each family was getting about 69 Palestinian pounds from the land. (Figure the pound at about $4.25.) By 1911 they were getting 77 pounds, but by 1938, the last year before the war boom began to affect prices, the income per family from the same land was 246 pounds per year.

Take a few of the milk production figures. In 1931 the dairies on this land produced 21 tons of milk. In 1941 they were getting 1,185 tons.

He had what he wanted—a plan for intensive farming to fit any farm in Palestine, hill or valley. He has new plans and some new crops. His chief crops for Palestine's farms are dairying, poultry, fruits, vegetables, small grains.

His newest crop successes are mangoes and avocado pears. The carob, or St. John's tree, which is a locust, was found to produce fruit equal in nutritive value to barley. It is a native tree which will produce two tons of its fruit per quarter-acre per year.

(In the spring of 1950 I met Dr. Volcani again. I went back to the magnificent scientific institute, where research in many important fields goes on, and then to the agricultural school for lunch where Dr. Volcani was waiting. We sat again at the same table and had once more a long, long talk about farming and what he had done and had planned for the future. More than any one man, I believe, he made possible the new Israel. I know there were the soldiers, the workers, the givers of lives and money, but had there not been his long research and his planning there would not have been the farms and the food and there would not be now any remote possibility of placing the newcomers on land had he not set up a formula which included knowledge of every inch of the land and what it would do. His son is with him now, in the field of science, and is doing much with the problem of minerals in the Dead Sea. I will always remember Dr. Volcani.)

There were experiments with grasses and with cross-breeding of fruits. In the classrooms, serious young men and women studied in advanced classes of agriculture. It was an exciting place.

In the citrus fruits research quarters was another remarkable person. Zdenka Samisch, a former Czech, with a fine, serious face and eyes, was chief of research.

She had, after introducing 20 varieties of olives, developed one which will replace the olive of Biblical days.

The latter is too small and its pit is too large. The new one will have a high oil content, is about twice as large and thus easier to harvest.

Citrus research (she studied at the University of California) is her chief work. She had spent five years meeting a challenge and had won.

All fruits have been dried or dehydrated save citrus.

Dr. Volcani produced what the modest feminine scientist had not shown us, her most successful product in the field of citrus research. It looked like a sheet of soft, orange-colored leather. Color glowed in it. It had a fine texture.

"The whole orange is here," he said, "juice, skin and pulp. Every bit of it is here."

He clipped off a piece of it. The taste was delightful. Mrs. Samisch showed how jellies, marmalades, even orange drinks could be made from it. There was no need for artificial flavor to be added. She had caught it. She had done the same for the lemon and grapefruit. That rich, warm-looking orange, rolled into a square of beautiful, soft material, can be shipped, kept on shelves, or in containers. It does not dry out. It would have been a godsend to Britain during the war. It will serve in far countries where fresh fruit is not readily available.

During the war, her method of extracting the essential oils brought in more than $500,000; 10 small factories are at work producing the concentrated juices of citrus fruits according to her method.

You left remembering her; knowing again that here was something going deep into the soil; deep into the life of the nation that already existed in the minds and hearts of those there. It was something built on work and intelligence, on sweat and long hours of work by head and hand.

Nearby was the Sieff Institute.

I talked with the director, Dr. Benjamin Block. He was from Poland. He had studied and worked in Prague, Brussels, Cambridge.

Out of his scientific research establishment had come millions of tablets of atabrine for the British Army and many other drugs which would not have been available for the Middle East and Africa but for this institute.

Out of this building had come the chemical plant at the Dead Sea where bromides, potash and magnesium are found in commercial quantities.

New petrol by-products have been discovered.

Five hundred scientists, driven from their home countries and attracted to Palestine by the drama of Zionism's planning and doing, are at work in the institute.

They have made some progress on the problem of leprosy, the ancient disease of the Middle East.

They are deep in a program of cancer research.

During the war, they literally saved the British war effort by discovering a new agent which enabled them to reclaim rubber without the hitherto necessary machines. They found a way to replace stainless steel as linings for vessels containing acids.

The story goes on and on.

In farming, in science and in industry, the roots were deep and sound. There was nothing ephemeral, nothing political. You knew, having seen this and some of the farms, that Zionism had builded on rock as strong and as solid symbolically as the rocks of Palestine's hills.

The doubts and the ideas I had entertained before arrival daily were being dissipated by evidence before my eyes. Whatever Zionism was, it was also a story of people. If that story was being projected against a screen of oil and power politics, it still did not remove the actual persons on the soil of Palestine. Even in a few days it was possible to see that here was a development and a rooted fact which would not be blown away by diplomatic double-talk, committee decisions or wishful thinking.

You went to bed with the smell of almond blossoms in the cool night air, planning for more of Palestine on the morrow.

6

"Heights of the Returning"

Rамот-Hashavim, Palestine
(1946)—At the gate, with the tall, furry pines about us, a middle-aged man, all dusty from unloading sacks of chicken feed, told us where we might find a settler who spoke English.

That is how I came to know, at this place which in English means, "The Heights of the Returning," one of a number of remarkable families.

I might have met William Stern and his tall, charming wife, Ilsa, in the foyer of the opera in Berlin in the early 1930s. Her father was one of the better-known financial successes of the city. Her husband's two businesses flourished.

But I met them here. William Stern came out of the large brooder-house, dusting his hands on his work-worn canvas pants. We went into his small but attractive dining room with colored prints of old masters and of new Palestinian artists on the wall.

We talked farming. I could have put him down at a county agents' meeting in Lyons, Ga., and he would have been right at home. I could have put him down for a discussion at the annual meeting of the Cherokee County (Georgia) Poultry Growers' Association and they would have listened to him with respect.

He is a farmer. And a good one.

The colony, a small-holders' group, owning their own land, is one of eight such in Palestine. Their stories are the story of William and Ilsa Stern and their children.

The story is this: What happens to middle-aged men and their families when they give up all they had, go to a strange land, learn a new language, and take up farming and poultry raising as a way of life?

All these men were middle-aged when they left Germany in

1933. Ten of them were lawyers. Fifteen were physicians. Some were pharmacists. Others were merchants and manufacturers. There were 60 families in all, each with children.

Dr. Volcani's comprehensive planning had anticipated such men.

"Poultry requires relatively little ground," said William Stern. "The work is that which can be done by middle-aged and old men who could not do the heavy work in the fields.

"But not a one of us had had any experience. Again, they wisely let us learn by doing. We were middle-aged and beyond. Therefore, it was not wise to send us to a school for a year or two. We had to establish homes and get our children in school. The only possible way to bring people of our age to agriculture is to put them to work, learning by their own work.

"We borrowed from the Agency to buy our land. It was expensive, not being hill land. But none of us bought to sell. I bought for my life and that of my family, perhaps for a second generation."

He gestured out the window to where a fine looking young girl with brown, wavy hair, clad in a pair of khaki trousers and a blue shirt, was pushing a wheelbarrow filled with equipment for the brooders.

"She," he said, "goes to an agricultural school."

William Stern talked very earnestly.

"So, we have chickens and we do vegetable and fruit farming. I found out one thing early. The Bible law about resting the land is true. Also I learned another thing: the peasant, or farmer, as you call him, must figure differently from a businessman. To be a farmer is another matter. The real farmer must do with self-work as far as is humanly possible. He must avoid hired work if he is to succeed. If I have to have a concrete wall built or special pipe laid I hire it, but I am the helper. Only those who work from early to late on farms can make a real living and assure their future."

That was real farm talk, the kind American farmers would understand—the talk of work.

The colony has done well. Each farmer is making a profit and has money in the bank. But it would not have done well without their co-operative effort. Each man owns his own land, does his own work, but he buys and markets through his co-operative. Had they tried to buy and sell individually, as so many communities of small American farmers do, they would have failed. Everything they buy comes through the co-operative.

William Stern pointed to the chicken pest which had struck them. He lost 1,300 chickens in 10 days. Thousands died in the colony. One man could do nothing. But the society got busy and had the best research done, hired the best poultry experts, and stamped it out. Then they had a meeting. They were independent owners, but they voted to share the loss evenly even though some had light losses and others heavy.

The co-operative has a few paid workers, five in all. They are those who do the marketing, buying and so on. The colony has built its own roads, schools, swimming pool and lighting system. It has its community hall for lectures, concerts, movies and so on.

Not one of the professional men who gave up being doctors, lawyers or pharmacists, not one of the businessmen, has deserted the farm colony.

I found myself thinking, as I looked at William Stern and his wife, that here were two persons who had known considerable wealth and what it would buy. They had given it up in their middle age to become farmers. And they liked it. Their children accepted it as their natural place in life—that of farmers.

Now, with the war done, they could go back to Germany and put in claims.

But none of them will.

"The agricultural factor in our minds, coming in the middle of our lives, has changed our minds and our lives," he said. "This is what we want to do and be."

I liked him. We sat drinking orange juice, poured from the tall pitcher which his wife had filled, and talking of lesser things. I met others from the colony. They all looked the picture of health.

Leaving, we met the smaller children coming from school. They were fit models for ads such as we know showing the healthiest of children eating various foods which, we are told, make them look as they do. These children had got it out of milk and fruit and wholesome farm food and out of the air and sun of Palestine. For them and their older brothers and sisters, there will be no wrench at middle age. They will grow up on the farms and take over from their parents.

We walked about the colony before we left, seeing the new chickens and preparations for others; going through the citrus groves; looking at the vegetable gardens with their marvelous big carrots and turnips and other vegetables.

It is a good life and a solid one. It had been taking root since 1933 and no wind of policies or violence will tear them up. They are there to stay, made strong by faith and, most of all, by work.

Going back down the shaded lane to the highway I knew I would never forget Ramot-Hashavin and its people. The translation of it, "The Heights of the Returning," was not merely symbolic.

By their work they had attained real heights in making two successful lives, one in the old Europe, another—the more difficult—in the new Palestine.

(On my return to Israel I went back to visit them. There was not time to let them know in advance. One day when we were passing near them Yitzhat and Joe took me there. The cypress trees along the entry road were larger and heavier. But the road was the same. There was again the sound of farm life and the smell of fields and flowers. Mrs. Stern was at the house and was good enough to remember me and to fetch more orange juice. She recalled our talk about Margaret Mitchell, whose book *Gone With the Wind* had charmed her as it had so many others in the world. She had not heard, somehow, of her tragic death by accident. The charming young daughter I had seen before is now married to a doctor and living in Jerusalem. William Stern was not at home. He was busy off obtaining some supplies, but Mrs. Stern showed me the new developments, the added poultry runs and the huge flocks of layers. A lot of work and progress were in evidence. She was hurrying to get things ready for a drive that afternoon to Tel Aviv where Koussevitsky was conducting the national symphony orchestra in one of his last performances there as guest conductor. All Israel was thrilled with him and he with it. The war had not touched them and I was glad. They had been among those about whom

I had thought often during the fighting.)

William Stern had said that his daughter attended an agricultural school. I knew such schools for young men. But for girls—- There was one nearby.

At Ayanot (Springs) Agricultural school for girls, we climbed stairways to the flat roof over one wing of the main building. Founded in 1929 it had achieved the appearance and productivity of a farm much longer established.

Girls ran it. They worked with tractors. They cleaned the stables, milked the cows, fed them, learned about butter fat content and so on. They cared for the poultry, the gardens, the bees and the fruit orchards. There were something more than 100 acres. They did the work of planting, tilling and harvesting.

A rather remarkable woman, Miss Zipora Ridelson, talked of the girls who had come from the concentration camps, from the partisan groups of Greece and Yugoslavia; of the girls from Syria and of Polish refugees from Iran. There had been difficulties of adjustment, but they were all at work and they had, somehow, rid themselves of most of their fears and terror. Work and the challenging promise of Palestine was the answer.

There were other days and other colonies. I remember one of them best of all because of the red-headed, blue-eyed, grinning Ukranian who was its chairman. There I saw families from Romania, Hungary, Bulgaria, Greece, Belgium and Italy. I saw them at work in the fields and shops, in the laundry, in the nursery and at meals and at play. The members had been there since 1932.

When they came they had no road. They occupied a hill in tents with marshes about them. Now the marshes were drained, good roads ran through them and a main highway was by their gate.

I was to see how other colonies had brought fine farms out of malarial marshes; out of swamps and hills. In the Jordan valley, in the Jezreel valley—all up and down Palestine—there were these farms. One I had asked especially to see.

Our road to it was through the hills of Ephraim, until at last we left the main highway and climbed one of the hills to arrive at Ein Hashofeth. Many of its farmers, they had told me, were

Americans.

I wanted to see how young men and women who had known nothing of concentration camps or terror; who had known the schools and the American way of life with its conveniences, its standard of living, would fit into the frontier, pioneer life of a hill farm in Palestine.

Harry Huberman, a Canadian, was in his office. He showed us the farm. Founded in 1937 with 130 members, it now has 147 plus 116 children, many of them born on the farm. On that vast hill and its slope they had 5,000 dunams, 2,000 in cultivation. The rest was being put into forests. Fruit, milk, eggs, vegetables of all kinds were their crops. They still were struggling, their notes were being met, the farm was just beginning to pay for itself.

That night, in my room, some of the Americans came and we talked. I met young men and women from New York, New Jersey, Detroit. Some had been students, teachers, and workers in factories and shops. There had been 90 of them.

Of that number, about a dozen Canadians and Americans had given up and gone back to their homes. But others had come to take their places. Those who had gone found the work too hard. To be suddenly put down in tents on top of a windy, harsh hill; to have Arabs murder two of them the first year and wound two others; to rise early and work late—all that had been a little too much.

The others had won through. Their faces showed it. The tents were gone. Good buildings, bath houses and kitchens were a part of their accomplishment. "We built a bath house before a dormitory or kitchen," they said, "and took a lot of teasing about being the clean Americans." Now, they were caring for some refugees. Cypress trees, wind, sun and stars made their hill beautiful by day and night.

I saw them at work with tractors, cultivators, trucks. I saw their hands hardened by work, their faces healthy and strong, their voices, as we talked, filled with belief in themselves and their future.

They, too, had found something their lives had never known before. They, too, along with the others, had found that by their work and planning a dream was taking substance before them.

They were a part of a new country. They were extending a new frontier. They are willing to work for it, and, like the others, to die for it if they must.

When we left the next morning the buildings were empty. Men and women were out at work. Joshua Leibner and his wife waited to say goodbye. The Americans fit into the picture as well as the others. (They still do today. I went back to see.)

7

Glass Blowers and Factory Workers

Haifa, Palestine (1946)—Out of the furnace came the big blob of molten glass. It was stuck on the steel tool held by the glass blower's helper. He spun it until the red mass of glass was shaped like a round loaf of bread. The blower got his tube well into it and then raised it to his lips.

The helper began to run, the glass pulling out into a tube which thinned out as the helper ran on. Up ahead, the blower danced around like a boxer, keeping that tube straight and air moving through it.

Back, back, ran the helper until the tube was stretched a full 60 feet. He stopped. Up in front the blower broke his blowing tube out of the glass. The helper removed his steel carrier. There lay a long, glistening tube which later was to be cut and made into ampules for drugs.

Already another blower and his helper were at work. There were three such teams and the long tubes were piling up there on the floor of the factory.

The glass blowers were big fellows, large enough to be good fast tackles on a big-time football team.

All about us the glass plant rumbled and hissed. Rollers smoothed out the panes of glass. Workers took it and cut it. Others packed it. Three shifts took the plant through each 24 hours.

I had seen a lot of industry and heard a lot about it at Tel Aviv. Here at Haifa were other plants which had helped win the British victory in Africa.

We went over to the Vulcan plant.

I was thinking on the way over that in America no one quite understood what went on in Palestine. The emphasis in too many articles had been on politics and oil. But here were people. I remember how many quite decent Americans had unwittingly taken the anti-Jewish propaganda line that Jews would not work with their hands; that they were good only in the soft jobs.

I had seen them calloused and muscled, tanned and hardened with many years of farm toil, on dozens and dozens of settlements which were monuments to their work and their intelligence.

Here were factories, and all the work, from sweeping the floors to the highly skilled jobs, was being done by Jews. The workers who fired the furnaces, who rolled the glass, who blew it, who made it into ampules or other articles in demand, were Jews, men and women.

You realized that what Nazi and world persecution had done was to funnel into Palestine some of the best minds, creative and directive, from almost every country of the world. You could see the impact of those minds on the country.

Amos Landman, secretary of the Solel Boneh Company, a co-operative which had built almost all the airfields of the Middle East, in addition to other military installations, took me to the Vulcan plant.

In the office of Zvi Lederer we had coffee. Lederer, plant manager, had been an officer in the Austrian army in World War I. After the war, he had come to Palestine as a farm settler. He soon demonstrated a genius for management. When World War II came along, they pulled him out of the farm to take over management of the Vulcan ironworks plant.

A big, broad fellow of middle age, with a fine broad face, we got along instantly. The Vulcan plant had been taken over when its former owners gave up the task of making it go. Lederer made it one of the great contributory plants in the British war effort.

In that plant they designed and made machines which could not be got to Palestine from Britain. They adapted machines to work never designed for them. Out of the research institute came plastics for moulding. Not being able to make forgings, they did such fine casting work that marine engines and diesels were able to use them and keep going. Without them, the war effort would have failed. Parts for generators on airplane engines were produced when they couldn't be got from Britain.

Here again—the workers who were busy with the moulds, the furnaces, the cranes, the pattern shop, the carpenter shop, the castings—all were Jews. Every imaginable sort of skill was there. The same was true at the rubber factory and at the ceramics plant, all close together in the Haifa Bay area. You realized that days before you had ceased to think of all the farmers and factory workers as Jews. They were just people and it came to you that this was the real idea behind the Palestine movement—they wanted to be a people. You remembered again the DP camp and Palestine again had a clear meaning.

You came to feel, too, how unrelated to reality was the fear of some of the Americans who long ago had ceased to think of themselves as Jews but as Americans, that a Jewish home would somehow disturb their political status. It would not, and going up and down Palestine you know it. This is the place for the homeless, for those who have no citizenship, no home. It is a place for the young Jews of any country where there is not opportunity. Here is a frontier. It challenges the dreaming and yearning of the young; it complements the hopes of the old. It can become a nation, but it will always be that kind of a nation— a place for those who need a land to which they can "belong."

Here in Haifa, with the atmosphere of the farms still fresh in your mind; with industry rumbling and thundering about you, you knew, too, that it was a fait accompli, that while misunderstanding and international double-dealing might slow it down, nothing could remove it.

Palestine lacks coal and metals. She has much of other raw materials. There may be oil in Palestine. It has not been explored. There is natural gas there, perhaps in sufficient quantity to use in industry.

At the Dead Sea, where plants are at work, there are unlimited deposits of potassium, bromide and their by-products. From the salt water will come unlimited magnesium. The chemicals already are processed in large quantities by the Palestine Potash Company.

There are an estimated 100,000,000 tons of phosphates in the area of Nebi Musa and the region east of Bethlehem. Bituminous limestone, gypsum, rock salt, sulphur, alum and other raw products are at hand in quantity.

Oil is available from nearby Iraq; Egypt has the cotton; Turkey and other neighboring countries could supply copper and other metals. Shipping could bring raw materials from all the world. Palestine easily could become a great industrial center which would re-make the entire Middle East.

Before the first World War, Palestine had almost no industry. The wineries and three soap factories of size, were about all. They and about 1,000 small home shops, employed perhaps five percent of the employed population. Today, in less than 30 years, there are 1,864 Jewish factories and plants, in addition to more than 10,000 small workshops, which employ about 25 percent of the Jewish population and produce goods valued annually at more than $100,000,000.

One of the best public relations men I ever met was H. Bochko, at Tel Aviv. Manager of the industrial exhibit, he talked well but backed it all with documented facts.

He, too, emphasized what soon becomes apparent to anyone willing to get out of Jerusalem and look. It is this—among those who have been coming to Palestine for the past 25 years are experts in all industrial fields. They have enabled Palestine to make fast industrial progress.

There are about 65,000 workers in industry. If each worker represents a family of a wife and child, then about 30 per cent of all the Jewish population makes its living from industry.

Examples of the variety of skills may be found in the fact that since 1937 a diamond-cutting industry, developed by refugees from Antwerp, now has 35 plants in Palestine employing 3,800 persons. All were trained in Palestine. The diamonds, mostly for industrial use, are purchased through the London diamond houses. Palestine, which builds its own machines for this trade, has become the fourth largest commercial diamond-cutting nation.

The pharmaceutical industry saw experts from Germany build it in 10 years to a production of more than 1,200 preparations and drugs.

Textiles, boots and shoes, bolts, pumps, fashions, precision instruments, metal industries, jams, marmalades, syrups, juices, and others of almost every field are represented.

During the war almost 50 percent of the total output went to the British Army.

The Palestine Electric Company, a Jewish triumph over the "it-can't-be-done-school," supplies electricity to all of Palestine save Jerusalem. There the British honor a franchise granted during the rule of the Turks.

About 60 percent of the Arabs are in agriculture. The ratio of Jews is the reverse. Therefore, one economy complements the other rather than competing.

As a result of Jewish industry and trade, Palestine's entire government largely is supported by taxes paid by Jews and Jewish industry. Jews pay an approximate two-thirds of all taxes levied. Yet the government pays for Jewish schools less than one-third the amount of support provided for Arab schools. Latest figures available were for 1943. The government spent $992,000 for an approximate 96,000 Arab children and $300,000 for 86,000 Jewish children. But the Jews don't complain. In 1943, they supported their educational system, including the universities and research stations, with more than $3,000,000. Never have I seen children provided with better school or health facilities.

Stories of at least two cities are familiar ones—those of Tel Aviv and Haifa. Tel Aviv has grown from a literally barren stretch of sand dunes into an urban center with more than 200,000 population. There are coffee houses, but there are more soda fountains, hamburger and hot-dog shops, ice cream shops and orange juice bars. There are shoe-shine parlors and also wandering vendors of shines with their boxes. Their hotels have bathrooms—with tub and shower.

Haifa grew naturally from the old city and now climbs atop Mount Carmel, where a beautiful, far-flung suburban community, with its own shops and stores, is developing. The rivalry between the two is intense. Tel Aviv has what amounts to a Jewish national theater, the Habima, an orchestra and the beginnings of a ballet. But Haifa, with its book-shops, its music and its beauty of sea and mountains, looks down its nose at Tel Aviv with a rivalry typical of American cities.

Their story is well known. What is not well known is the growth of small towns and villages. They were Arab villages.

Now they are Arab and Jewish. The Arabs still are there. Those who tried are in better homes, wear better clothes, own their own places. They were among those who went calmly along, ignoring the boycott called in Egypt against the Jews in Palestine. There are many such villages.

For the Arab farmer, they have become markets for his vegetables, his lambs, sheep, goats and beef, and, to be factual, for his pork. There are among the Jews in Palestine a small percentage of the orthodox, a larger percentage which is religious but not orthodox, and a still greater number which respect the teachings but do not follow them in entirety. Nothing could be more wrong than to imagine that a Jewish national home in Palestine would mean a state religion. The first to oppose such an idea would be the Jews.

These small villages have garages, in the American manner; restaurants, shops and invariably at least one or more small plants. So do many of the actual farm communities. Coming from the South, and knowing that one of the problems there is to provide small manufacturing plants for farm communities to give off-season employment to any of the population not needed on the land, it was interesting to see how well it worked.

There is a plan to keep a balance between industry and agriculture. The absorptive capacity of the land and industry carefully is measured. There is room for at least 1,000,000 more Jews in industry and agriculture in Palestine and not a single Arab would be displaced or economically reduced. Indeed, as the eyes may see, the Arab in Palestine who already looks better clothed and fed than in any other Arab country, would be the more improved in living standards.

I think the Arab knows it.

He keeps pouring into the land, illegally when he can't come otherwise, despite the Arabic politicians who send out propaganda about how hard is his lot in Palestine.

8

"It Will Not Be Blown Away"

J ERUSALEM, Palestine (1946)—Consider the real issue of Palestine as it is.

Remove the oil from its face.

Banish the unworthy "now-is-not-the-time-isms" in which the lethargic and fearful indulge.

Lay bare the selfishness of those who, for exploitation purposes, would keep the Near East in status quo.

Shut out the huffing and puffing from the arena where the power-politics wrestling match is under way.

Ignore the unreality of any Arab military uprising.

Analyze—and dismiss—the thoroughly unsubstantiated argument that there isn't room for more people.

Forgetting the prejudices, the smoke-screens, the wishful thinking, stripped of all intangibles and inconsequences, what remains of the issue?

There remains a sharply-etched, living and breathing, hard-working and productive, deeply-rooted Jewish life all up and down Palestine. It will not be blown away by the gales of power politics. It will not be trampled out by any imagined attack because it is too strong and it has, should the need arise, a core of ex-soldiers who fought for Britain, who remember dead comrades left behind, who will fight for them and themselves if the need should come.

It is there. It has demonstrated beyond any argument that it is workable. It has proved to be practical by any standard of measurement.

It already is an agricultural and industrial success to the degree it could become the basis for a great rennaissance of learning, of modern farming and industry to inspire and lift the standards of all the Middle East.

There is enough room for immigration limited only by the recommendations of the Jewish Agency. This Agency, composed of half Zionists and half non-Zionists, certainly would not be so foolish or ill-advised as to bring in those for whom there was not room and not a selected place. Even the Arabs or the most rabid anti-Zionist would not make such a claim.

Then, too, it must be kept in mind this is by no means essentially a political problem. Political Zionism itself does not agree in all matters, as do not other political groups. This is primarily and entirely a problem of persons, displaced, homeless and wretched.

The fanatical mobs who marched, hoarse with shouting, against the world, demonstrated that in times of war they will act bloodily and brutally from passions drawn from mythology or from slogans produced by the twisted philosophy of fuehrers. They were by no means all members of the Nazi party who so marched.

If 80 percent of the Jews in the displaced persons camps have, despite the horror through which they lived, been able to do the astounding thing of creating a new dream for themselves and their future, it is inconceivable the world will lack the integrity to give it a chance. And 80 percent of the Jews in the Allied zone in Europe do want to go to Palestine. Perhaps the figure is higher. But certainly it is that high.

But there is not room?

Why push the Arabs around?

Why should the Palestine Arab bear the brunt of such immigration?

Let's take them one by one, although one answer will serve them all.

There is room. I have seen it. I have driven through the hills and valleys. I know what I saw. There are bare hills for hour on hour. There are empty valley slopes and some valley land itself goes untilled, traversed now and then by wandering Bedouin flocks.

Being farm born, I know a little something of land and land uses. I saw enough idle, unused land to take care of several thousands of new persons. They would not crowd a single Arab.

That is not all.

In the south of Palestine is the Negeb. It alone could take, once the water is brought there, three-fourths of the Jews in the Allied zone were the British willing to turn it over to the Jewish Agency for development and the bringing to it, as the land was ready, of immigrants.

It already has been tested. Land was bought near Beersheba in 1941. Since 1941, three outposts in the Negeb have carried on investigation and research. Water, soil, climate, possible plants and cultivation have been studied by some of the best experts in these fields.

It is important to keep in mind the solution to the problem of Palestine is not theoretical or political. It is a well thought-out, scientifically-planned program. There are some 3,000,000 acres in that vast region where once ancient cities and civilizations flourished. Not all of them would come under cultivation. The work of research still goes on. But enough is known already to make practical the use of vast areas of that land. It is not a true desert. It is soil, not sand. The desert needs only water to blossom as have other areas in Palestine formerly classified "desert."

Dr. Walter Clay Lowdermilk, of America, made a long study of Palestine. His findings are published and have been a best-seller to those interested in the problem. One of America's best-known agronomists, his study was factual, nonpartisan.

Many other experts, interested scientifically, have sustained this view of soil experts and of political experts.

Palestine is, of course, small. Its 10,429 square miles would go about five times into my home state of Georgia. It is about the size of Vermont. It is about 1/38 the size of Egypt; a mere 1/100 the size of Ibn Saud's relatively empty Saudi Arabia; and approximately 1/17 the size of Iraq.

It maintains without trouble its present population of about 1,600,000. The population roughly may be divided as follows: Moslems, 1,000,000; Jews 500,000, and Christians 130,000. The figures run a little higher, but these are approximate.

The Transjordan, a part of Palestine proper, was made by the British into a separate state. It is roughly three times as large as Palestine; has good land, yet sustains a population of about 350,000 persons.

That Britain should be in the process of granting to this loosely held state full independence and official recognition, while withholding adequate immigration from Palestine, is one of the fantastic contradictions and more bitter ironies of the present situation.

I have purposely refrained from more than casual comment about Britain's part. In the first place, it has been covered adequately in many newspaper articles, books and magazines. Palestine was given to Britain under mandate by the now defunct League of Nations for the express purpose of developing it as a haven for Jews. The Balfour Declaration of November 2, 1917, officially committed the British Government to establishment of a national home for the Jewish people . . . "without prejudicing the civil and religious rights of non-Jewish communities . . . or the rights and political status enjoyed by Jews in any other country."

Under the late Neville Chamberlain, who disastrously took every road of appeasement open to him, this declaration was nullified. Britain holds her mandate under definite legal shadow. The League which granted it no longer exists. It is one of the tragedies of the postwar world that Britain, which has so fine a record of defending liberty and freedom and human rights generally, should have traveled the road of appeasement, fear and moral wrong in Palestine.

Palestine is historically a Jewish nation. The Jews were there originally and they never entirely left. The Arabs have been there in greater numbers for many centuries. Under them and the Turks, the "land of milk and honey" washed away, was plundered by armies, and became a semiarid land of goat herds and villages.

No one wants to remove the Arabs. There is room for them and for all the immigrant Jews who need a homeland.

But what claim does the Arab leadership have on a world which gave enormously of its lives, blood and treasure to insure freedom and human dignity?

Nothing at all. Generally speaking, and with some few exceptions, the Arab either openly favored the Nazis and the Japanese or was a theoretical neutral. He worked to defeat the Allies. His enemy aid contributed to the death of many Allied soldiers, American and English.

The Jews produced not merely from field and factory. Of nearly a million Palestine Arabs, hardly 7,000 enlisted. Of about a half million Jews almost 30,000 were in British uniforms.

The driver of the car which took me over the country lost a son in a Commando raid. The story of the Palestinian girl, Hannah Szenes, is already a legend. She was dropped into Hungary by parachute to do a special job of intelligence. She was captured, but only after she had done her job. The Nazis shot her. There were many others who did similar jobs.

There were many thousands of Jews in the armies of the world. Here in Palestine, in school and settlement, I saw young boys who had fought all through the occupation of Greece, Czechoslovakia and Yugoslavia as partisans.

Also, here in Palestine, the British and Jews were rationed during the war, as were Americans and English. But not the Arabs. They would not agree.

The Arabs were the eager aids and agents of Germany in the Middle East. Until 1941, the Arabs threatened to sell their oil to the Germans. They tried to revolt in behalf of the Germans in Iraq and had to be put down with arms. In Palestine, the Grand Mufti fled to his friends, the Germans. The loyalty of the Arab leadership to the concept of liberty must be bought.

Yet, it is not the Arab farmer, shopkeeper or herdsman who blocks the way. It is the rich and mostly absentee feudal landlords, the princes, the pashas, the religious leaders who now beat their breasts for the Atlantic Charter.

But what do the simple, everyday Arabs think of the Jews? Are they, the Jews, driving them out of Palestine?

Before the first World War, before the mandate to Britain and before the Turks were driven out—there were only 450,000 Moslems in Palestine and some 55,000 Jews. By the time the second world war came along and the Jews had for 25 years been "crowding the Arab out of Palestine," there were 930,000 Moslems in the country and 445,000 Jews.

You hear a lot about the Jews who try illegal entry into Palestine. But nothing at all about the hundreds of Arabs who enter illegally because they know that in Palestine the lot of the Arab in standard of living and education and health is, because of the Jews, better than anywhere else. The facts give lie to the general propaganda.

There are many who honestly oppose a Jewish home in Palestine. Certainly they are not anti-Semitic. They are uninformed, believing it would create for them difficulties and disturb their own nationality. It would not do so. They are simply mistaken. Has the Irish Free State disturbed an Irishman in any other country where he holds citizenship? There are others who are callously unaware or disinterested.

The solution, as it seems to me, is for Palestine to be immediately opened to immigration by the homeless ones of Europe and then be mandated to the UNO as a Jewish national home within which the Arab shall have every right and privilege accorded others. Partition is not merely wrong, but patently unworkable.

And this must be done now. Committees cannot arrive at any other solution.

Until it is done, there can be no real beginning at solving the whole problem of peace. And justice and morality, I think, are weary of waiting on fear and appeasement of error. (So I wrote in 1946.)

9

The Years Between

Let this brief chapter of the years between visits be something of the story of Yitzhak, which is Hebrew for Isaac. He and I became fast friends with a like enthusiasm for houmus, Arab bean-butter eaten with the flat Moslem bread which, when torn, makes convenient cones for scooping. With it go spring onions and garlic-dill pickles. We liked, too, the gefulta fish at Metulah, the fresh fish at Tiberias, or the Sea of Galilee, and herring with fresh onions for breakfast. In a few days I had known Yitzhak all my life.

He had been a sergeant in the Polish army, had been taken by the Russians and put into a labor camp. He was there for four years. When the Communist-dominated Polish government was established, he and others were given orders to report back for service in his old country.

He made his way through underground channels to Palestine, arriving there at about the time the birth pains of the new nation were beginning. These had begun in 1945. By 1946 they had become frequent.

The British Labor Government, which long had favored the homeland plan, was led from blunder to blunder by Prime Minister Ernest Bevin, whose decisions to this day are not really understandable. Out of them came the necessity for force and terror. Sabotage by the Irgun and Stern groups and military sabotage by the Palmach (attack) group of the Haganah went steadily on, growing in daring and volume as did retaliation. The blowing up of government buildings in the heart of Jerusalem, the incredible daring by which a wing of the King David Hotel was destroyed, the awesome terror which matched British terror and reached into Europe to do so, could not be stopped,

although the British increased the number of their troops and
police to huge numbers. Illegal entry of immigrants was also
stepped up.

Of all this, Yitzhak was a part. He has yet today two bullets
in his body. He was typical of the courage and resourcefulness
of the time. He had a job by day. He was subject to call any
night. He was often one of those wading out to a dark, silent
ship to carry ashore some immigrant. These immigrants were
taken to houses in the neighborhood, often children in arms,
or old men carried on the backs of those assisting.

"We would knock on a door," Yitzhak recalls. "When the door
was answered, there we would be with an immigrant, wet, without possessions, usually speaking a language not understood by
the person at the door.

" 'Who is he?' would be the whisper.

" 'I don't know his name. He is a Jew.'

"The immigrant would be admitted. The door would close.
By the time word of the ship's arrival leaked out, these new
arrivals would be hidden."

Sometimes the Irgun or Haganah men in such work would
have to run through the dark. One morning Yitzhak arrived
home with a bullet in his leg. It was bandaged, he put on fresh
clothes and went to his job. There were many such nights. He
was one of many such men. All Jews were acting as voluntary
intelligence agents and partisan workers.

In 1946 an effort was made to liquidate the Haganah by arrests
and to collect all arms held by Jews. Once that was done, Britain
planned to establish an Arab state with a protectorate status.
Jews would have a minority status with guaranteed "rights."
By July of 1946 there were thousands of the leading Jews in
jails and camps. Farm settlements were searched for arms.

Out of this developed a game of hide and seek. A truck would
arrive at a farm and take away all arms. Police would come and
search. When they were gone, the truck would return with its
cargo. Only now and then would police find arms above the
few legally licensed for repelling Arab raids, which had made
the Jewish farm settlements similar to frontier outposts endan-
gered by Indian war parties in the early history of our own

country.

Early in 1947 the United Nations appointed a new Commission. This was the 19th named to "study and report." Partition was recommended. Britain rejected this, still duped by the Arab league politicians who still talked of an all-Arab Middle East. Partition nevertheless was carried by a narrow margin in a November 29th test.

Until debate had begun in October, violence, terror and death were a part of the daily news ration.

After the partition vote, Arabs began guerilla warfare on a large scale. British administration during this period was particularly shortsighted. The vote which had gone against them caused them to bend an ear to those who said, "Get out. Quit Palestine. The Jews will fight each other when the Irgun and the Stern gangs meet to see which one can take over. You will not be gone more than two weeks before you will be called back."

Massacres, many of them with more than twenty persons killed, became frequent.

Yitzhak was one of those in this fighting. He was an expert man with grenades and was unusually daring. He penetrated often deep into Arab villages to blow up buildings housing arms or village leaders whose men had massacred Jewish settlers.

In March of 1948, the British began to pull out. A few weeks before, ministers of seven Arab states—Syria, Iraq, Lebanon, Transjordan, Egypt, Saudi Arabia, and the Yemen—had met in Cairo and pledged themselves to give aid and to march against the Jews when the British should leave.

Guerilla war had been going on without ceasing. By March it was total war. The success of the Haganah and the two terrorist groups was unexpected. The Arabs were hurried out of some cities by their leaders with the word that they would be back in two or three weeks to loot Tel Aviv, Haifa and all other Jewish centers. They were driven from other towns by the fighting for territory.

The tempo of war increased. The 40 million Arabs of the attacking states were represented by about 40 thousand soldiers. They were not eager to fight. They were illiterate and badly trained. They did have some modern equipment. The Jews in the beginning had none at all. In the hills around Lake Hulah on down into Galilee and south into the desert, war raged, ranging from sniping to guerilla raids to battles of scale.

On May 14 the government and nation of Israel were proclaimed. "Official" war began shortly thereafter.

Arab armies marched into Israel on May 15, 1948. Between May and June 1st an Egyptian force had by-passed farm settlements in the desert into the Jewish coastal belt at Gaza. A second column, marching through Arab territory, reached the southern edges of Jerusalem. In the north, the Jews took Acre, succeeding where Napoleon had failed, and advanced along the coast to the Lebanon frontier at Ras en Nakura. Attacks by Syrians and Lebanese in Galilee and the Jordan valley were halted. The toughest fighting was in the Old City of Jerusalem and along the Jerusalem-Tel Aviv road.

The United Nations tried to find a formula for peace. The Arabs twice rejected "cease fire" proposals, with the Jews each time accepting. The Arab Legion continued to shell the Jewish quarter of the Old City, and supply of arms continued to the Arab armies. Heavy fighting continued for control of the Jerusalem-Tel Aviv road.

This was the time of the spectacular but disastrous attack on Latrun, British police station occupied by Arabs, from which the road could be dominated.

"In that battle," remembered Yitzhak, who had a magnificent combat record in the Israeli army, "there were kids right off boats from DP camps. They spoke Hungarian, or most of them did. The officers we had couldn't speak their language. More than 200 were killed and the attack beaten off. But we kept the road open."

On May 31, Count Bernadotte arrived for the United Nations and began seeking a truce. This he obtained on June 11, but fighting broke out again four weeks later. A second truce was agreed to on July 18. On September 17, Count Bernadotte was murdered.

The Sternists are blamed for that tragedy, but few in Israel believe them guilty. An outside power is suspected as having arranged it.

Ralph Bunche, the American mediator, at last established a truce, in a magnificent diplomatic triumph which raised American and UN prestige.

In October the Israeli troops moved into the unoccupied Negeb, where they still are.

The next chapters were written from Israel. They do not attempt to tell the full story. They are impressions of the people and their spirit and they do reveal, I hope, something of the character of the new nation.

10

A Long Way in 31 Hours

JERUSALEM—It is a long way to a lot of places and one of them is Jerusalem. I had made it before, but always with nice breaks in between at Rome, Athens or Cairo. This time there was no break. From New York the big Constellation droned through the night to Gander, Newfoundland, and landed on an ice-covered runway, with snow falling gustily.

There was an hour there in the old transport building built by American soldiers for the great flocks of our planes which took off there for the Atlantic crossing during the war. It is a quiet place now, with a small milk bar, a real bar and restaurant and the same old hard benches.

We took off in the snow, the propellers flinging it back in hard-driven lines. Ahead of us was the Atlantic. Dawn came in three hours, but it was four more before we broke through the overcast near the shore of Ireland and went on across the land to the big airport at Shannon. From Gander to Shannon was seven hours. It was past noon in Shannon, and we had lunch of steak and kidney pie and stood awhile in the warm Irish sun until the flight was called.

Three and a half hours afterward there was Paris and Orley Field with dusk coming on fast. Two and a half hours later there came Zurich, Switzerland, with big glasses of cold milk for sale at the airport bar in a building antiseptically clean.

There followed one of the hours which make travel worthwhile. From the Zurich airport the plane had to climb to 20,500 feet for the flight across the Alps.

So tightly held by mountains was the airport the climbing had to be done in great spiraling circles. But at last the altitude was attained and the ship turned across the Alps.

It was about 10 o'clock. Back home it was only 4 in the afternoon. There was a bright, full moon shining through a sky
which was almost cloudless. The great peaks of the Alps reached
up darkly toward us, but as we looked down we could see the
moonlight spread across the snow-covered slopes of the peaks and
ridges, making it white and gleaming like a vast Christmas dream
gone mad. As far as we could see, the moon painted the mountains white, making the snow live and glow with the peculiar
silver of the reflected light from the distant, dead planet. In
almost every valley there were small villages, making their pres-
ence known by their tiny points of electric lights. Sometimes
these were seen clinging to the sides of towering peaks. They
were the Christmas lights in the tremendous expanse of snow-
covered peaks. I would not have been surprised had Santa Claus
and his reindeers gone by outside the plane's windows.

Once past the Alps we flew on over Italy, seeing the lights of
Milan at our left, and landed, finally, at Rome's Cimpino airport.
The GI's who served in Italy will remember it. In 1945 there
were wrecked buildings all about it. Even now, the planes still
taxi up on the old metal landing strips which the Americans put
down. But now the airport building is enlarged and includes
even one of those weird "expresso" coffee machines which look
like nothing else save one of Rube Goldberg's "inventions."

There at Rome we changed to a DC-4 for the seven-hour
nonstop flight across the Mediterranean to Lydda, not far from
Tel Aviv in the new state of Israel. There were head winds and
it stretched to eight and a half hours.

It was almost fantastic to think that on Sunday evening at 8
we had left New York and now, 31 hours later, including stops,
were putting down at a town only 40 miles from old Jerusalem.

There was excitement in it for me. I had seen it in 1945 and
more thoroughly in 1946 and now I was coming back again. But
I didn't even look out the window. I was watching the passen-
gers—the old woman who had got out of Czechoslovakia; another
who sat weeping silently . . . the old rabbi with the square-cut
white beard who clutched in his hand a bottle of sacramental
wine given him by friends at Paris; the small, dumpy woman
who was singing a Zionist song, and the others to whom the

landing meant a dream, long-dreamed, now coming true. The
ship circled and came in and when the wheels touched and I
released the belt I suddenly knew I was very, very tired. There
had been two consecutive nights in those 31 hours and with the
help of barbiturates I had slept perhaps four hours in the whole
time.

Friends met us and we had coffee in the airport restaurant,
waiting for transportation, and I watched again a sight one sees
nowhere else—birds flying in at the windows and picking up
crumbs from the tables and floor.

The air was soft and fresh from a rain that had fallen a half
hour before. I sat there, relaxing and looking, and remembering
how it had been when I had landed there before in a shaky old
Anson with fabric covered wings, one of the planes of the
Egyptian National Airlines, long obsolete and dating to about
1935. The British, irritable, nervous and burdened with their
unrationalized sense of guilt, were in charge. I understood them
and felt a little sorry for them as human beings caught in the
chain of events.

About us now was the excited clamor of conversation as rela-
tives and friends come to greet arrivals on our plane, began to
steer them through customs. English, Yiddish and Hebrew were
mingled in it.

Our dubious coffee finished, we moved out into the sun and
to the parked car. . . .

Around Lydda Airport, which is the port for Jerusalem and
Tel Aviv, there were the rolls of old, rusting barbed wire and
slit trenches fallen in. There had been fighting about it in the
war which began on the evening of May 14, 1948, when the
British troops withdrew and the Arab armies began to move
against the Israeli forces. I had seen it last in the terrorist days
of 1946. Then it was but 40 miles to Jerusalem. It still is. But
that road can't be used because part of it lies in Arab territory,
their troops holding it when the truce was signed in February
of 1949. It is 60 miles now by a diverse route.

Along the way we passed many places where men had died
fighting. Along one stretch of the road we saw more than 20
burned-out wrecks of trucks destroyed by Arab guns and mortar

fire from the ancient hills above. It was the stretch called the Burma Road, Bab El Wad, the life-line from Jerusalem to Tel Aviv. There were villages with buildings destroyed by shellfire. There were bridges down by demolition. There were more signs of war than I had imagined. In 1946 I had been shocked by the irony of so many tanks and soldiers in the Holy Land. Now, to see old gun emplacements, heavily sandbagged, and to come upon shell-shattered buildings and old trenches, was even more of a paradoxical reality. The damage is more than I had thought. It was, in a sense, a small war, but with modern weapons, even a few of them, no war is small. Men died in the days of bows and arrows and they die even more easily now in the days of machineguns and artillery.

There is always a terrible loneliness in old deserted trenches and gun emplacements where the wind hunts, blowing the rags of old sand bags. These places are lonely because they have known the enormous vitality of high resolve and courage; fear and death, and the immortal towering moments when man is at his best or worst. Old battlefields large or small, always seem empty and lonely.

Somewhere along the way we came, the Nazarene had walked in the old days long gone. Before that His mother had come that way on the way to Bethlehem where she found a stable to sleep and her Son was born. They had passed Roman forts and seen the sun on the armor and eagles of the legions.

Now, we drove along beside the signs and scenes of war. A gentleman with us, an Israeli, talked and pointed them out.

"We lost 40 men storming that hill . . . the guns from the peak there commanded the road . . . there was hard fighting here, because this point was one of the major defenses of Jerusalem. . . . Had they taken this they could have moved on into the city with their tanks."

One could almost see the mocking figure of an old Roman Centurian standing by the road, smiling sardonically, and saying: "It has always been so here. They still dig up our bones who followed Caesar and the Eagles of Rome."

But, at last, we reached a hilltop and ahead could see Jerusalem on her hills, her red and tan roofs dull under heavy clouds.

It always is a great sight. Her minarets, her church and monastery spires send their graceful heights above the buildings below. Behind them stretch the Judean hills and, beyond them, almost hidden by the blue haze, the mountains of Moab, where an unknown, lonely grave holds all that is mortal of Moses.

Driving through the city I was again appalled by the destruction; the more impressive because so much has been restored. Many buildings, left whole, still bear the scars of shrapnel and mortar pieces. In the Palestine Post, where I borrowed a typewriter to do these pieces, the city room ceiling is pitted with deep holes and gashes where fragments of mortar shells had come through the shattered windows. There are many signs of war.

The Arab forces of Transjordan hold now the Old City of Jerusalem. In the very first hour of arrival in Jerusalem we climbed up ladders to the roof of the war-shattered Hospice of Notre Dame and looked down into the Old City where the Arab Legion stood guard on the walls. Beside us stood the Israeli soldiers, with loaded rifles and fixed bayonets. The truce is being kept. But, from the roof there a good broad jumper could almost leap from Israel into the Old City. There are many points closely held.

On the roof a big raw-boned Polish soldier, veteran of the fighting that had raged there, stood and looked with us into the old city and at the Arab Legionaires on guard.

In his halting English he asked me about America and tried to understand some of the impressions obtained from movies and the gossip of soldiers' camps and barracks.

He shook his head unbelievingly at my analysis of America. "This is my place," he said, sweeping an arm toward the horizon. "This is my country."

The Old City is old enough, but it is not really very old. It was built in 1526 by Suleiman the Magnificent, the Turkish commander who pushed the Crusaders out of the Holy Land. Many persons persist in thinking of it as the city Christ knew, and many devout pilgrims come to the holy places. Their authenticity is in doubt. The Via Doloroso Christ is beneath many feet of rubble, as Jerusalem was destroyed four times after the Crucifixion. All that matters not at all, of course, since it is what happened there, the Crucifixion and the Resurrection, which means so much to Christians the world over. It is not really greatly important to fix exact spots save for tourist business. It is a city holy to Christians, Jews and Arabs. The more devout Jews are greatly troubled today because they cannot pray at the Wailing Wall, part of the Mosque of Omar, sacred to the prophet. And Christians yearn to see and pray at the Church of the Holy Sepulchre.

That first night as I went early to bed I turned out the lights and looked out through the wide-open windows at the moonlight shining on the walls and minarets of the Old City, not more than 100 yards from my window. I could see the moonlight on the towers and saw it catch, too, the bayonet of a guard on the walls. It was a beautiful sight, heavy with a sense of history and of great events. I turned out the light and went to bed. It was very quiet. Jerusalem turns in early.

The next morning I was awakened early and as I lay listening I could hear, deep in the Old City, a rooster crowing loudly. I wondered if he were a lineal descendant of that cock which had crowed at Peter's denial of his Lord, but even as I wondered, I went back to sleep to awake again at 10. A man sleeps long after 31 hours on a plane—if he is lucky.

11

"Out of the Blood and Dying"

J ERUSALEM—After breakfast on
that first morning of my return to Jerusalem, I came back to my
room in the King David Hotel, put my typewriter on the table,
put on my pajamas, put paper in the machine and tried to think
out something to put on that sheet of paper.

I had seen this Israeli nation striving to be born four years
before. It had caught me up as few things have done. I had
stayed at isolated farm settlements where I had been issued a
rifle. And I knew it wasn't for fun. When you see one of the
rocky hills of Israel, of Palestine, as we then called it, you know
how lonely they can be. I knew, too, they didn't put gun slits
in the blockhouses for nothing, although at the time there was
in existence an unofficial truce.

I was a man who as a kid had come up on our frontier
tales. And then, on a sudden, there was I in one of the oldest
lands of the world with my suitcase packed with $3 shirts and
good underwear, tooth paste, safety razor blades and so on, trying
to sleep in a room with rifle slits in the concrete wall and a rifle
leaning against my bed with live ammunition in it. There was
always then a bare chance of an Arab attack. One could end
up with me very dead indeed and while the odds were it would
not come there was no escaping the fact it might. There I was,
a man even then in my early 40s, all of a sudden given a chance
to live in the old frontier days when the Indians might attack.
I loved it.

But when it was done, and the Arabs had not attacked, and
days later I was just a 40-year-old-plus guy waiting for the train
from Lydda to Cairo, I tried to reason it out. I knew those Jewish
youngsters and their older counterparts were people I liked. Not

since our own frontier days had there been such an experiment. They went to work in the fields with their rifles as one of their work tools. I was for them. I knew they had plenty of courage and would fight. I knew they were working as hard as any persons in the world. I had chosen to visit chiefly the farmer settlements. I knew them to be good farmers. I knew, too, that too many persons had never heard of a Jewish farmer or factory worker or laborer. I saw plenty of both.

That was 1946. When I got to Lydda on the train down from Jerusalem, and was transferring to the Cairo sleeper, an Arab baggage porter in a dirty old robe, a soiled "K'fyia" (head cloth) and "aghalia" (black cords which bind it on), suddenly looked at the darkening sky, put down my bags and, having no prayer rug, climbed on a platform bench and banged his head in his prayers toward Mecca.

"Brother," I thought, "you are not a bad fellow but you don't know from nothing, and you are being used by persons smarter than you, who are exploiting your religion for their own ends. I have seen that at home, too."

I thought then that if the fighting came, as I believed it would, the Jews of Palestine would fight well. But I also feared the British-trained and equipped Arab Legion of Transjordan would be the balance of power that would defeat the Palestinian forces.

Well, the time came when the people with rifles by their beds had to pick them up and fight. There were some of those isolated farm settlements which were wiped out by the Arabs and the bodies mutilated. The war came. For a time it hung in the balance. The Arabs should have won because they had the most soldiers, the most guns, the most planes. But the Jewish soldiers won and let it be set down in complete honesty there were never better or braver soldiers.

One of these days I want to write a story about a Quixotic night charge on the ancient Jaffa gate of old Jerusalem in which there were a crippled man and a girl running in the dark toward that gate. The story will wait. It will come later.

Out of the blood and the dying came a new nation called Israel. It replaces the one destroyed 586 B. C. by an Assyrian general from Babylon called Nebuchadnezzar. In a sense it is a nation risen from the dead after more than 2,000 years.

It is a nation which won in somewhat the manner of Deborah, that great woman who welded the tribes together and defeated the Canaanites on the Plains of Armageddon, or the Jezreel (Israel) Valley. Today those plains are dotted with the farms and small-holder settlements of Jews from many, many nations.

The Government is new. The industries are new. Imports are 10 times that of exports. There isn't much to export save citrus, diamonds finished by the expert cutters who are refugees here, and certain textiles and crafts.

Immigrants have come in the number of 370,000 since May, 1948.

There is no time to become a small, balanced nation with a balanced budget. There are always new people. Schools, hospitals and all demands of services are quadrupled.

America has helped build this nation.

There will be need for America to help for years.

But there is a tendency to say that the nation now is formed; the Arabs are defeated and that the nation can carry on. When the decision was one illustrated by the gun kept by the bed, it was easy to give money. When everything seemed against the formation of a Jewish home land, hands reached eagerly to pockets. Now there are those here saying the Americans forget too soon; they gave money when it didn't hurt. These are the extremists. I know it isn't true. I know the hundreds who gave until it hurt, who did without to give to the hope of a new Israel, a new nation risen from the ancient ashes.

It is here. I believe it is important to the world. It needs help even more than in the days before there was a nation. It is important to Jew and Gentile alike that the manning of Israel be understood.

I went back to my window and looked out on the garden in the rear of the hotel and, beyond its dark, bordering cypresses, to the nearby walls of the Old City.

Beyond were the dark masses of brooding cypresses about the Garden of Gethsemane. To the left were the hills where the Crucifixion and Resurrection had taken place.

Here was the place where, as some gifted writer had said, "the heresy of One God had become a vital faith." On one of these hills was an ancient village mentioned in old tablets dating to 1,400 B. C. Here Solomon built a temple to that one God, Yahweh (Jehovah). Here came Nebuchadnezzar; the glittering hosts of Persians, the Romans, the Turks, who were there for almost 800 years; the gentle Allenby, walking on foot into the city from which he had driven the Turks, and finally the troops with the Star of David on their flag, bloodily defending their half of the hill and the new city to hold it for the capital of the new Israel.

It has always been a nervous city. Twanging bows, or mortar shells—the city and the hills know both of old.

Now, it is strangely the cradle of the Western culture in the Middle East, which culture is based on the Christian ideal as evolved from Judaism. As once had been born there the heresy of One God, which became a faith, now in the city is being revealed the meaning of the dignity of man; the Western concept of government which is of, for and by the people, and not a feudal despotism, exploiting the people.

Around Jerusalem and Israel were the hostile Arab states, licking their wounds, embittered and fearful. They were fearful four years before. If they could not put that fear into words, they understood it just the same. They saw Arabs watching Jewish tractors at work. They noted the attention paid to children and the old by the Jewish settlers while Arab children and the aged were neglected and subjected to the oppressive physical and social pressures of extreme poverty.

Seeing, they also could hear the termites of change gnawing away at the feudal foundations beneath them. So, they hated and they feared. Their rumors stirred the religious fanatics.

Now, the former Jewish object lesson of western culture and civilization is a nation. All may see it and witness its meaning. It stands there in the wretchedness of the Middle East, as a continuing irrefutable denial of the Soviet propaganda that Western ways were not good for the working people, the little people, of the world. That we must all remember.

The telephone rang. An information officer was waiting in the lobby. It was time to go.

12

The Farm and the Fort

J ERUSALEM—Less than a 10-minute drive from the capital of Israel there is a hill called Ramat Rahel, "The Hill of Rachel." The tomb of that excellent woman is on its slope, hard by the road to Bethlehem.

The hill curves back from the road and at its northern end there is a long-established "kibbutz," or farm settlement made by the Zionists some years ago. The word kibbutz means "a collection."

When the war began it was a thriving farm collective community. It had 100 cows, about 12,000 chickens, gardens and a laundry which did some of the business for Jerusalem and earned money for the settlement.

Because of its position by the Bethlehem-Jerusalem road, it became a focal point of war. At the outset of the fighting which followed hard on the heels of the departing British it was held by its own people reinforced by some "home guard" soldiers sent out from Jerusalem.

One day, from the rock hills beyond, and from the ridge above the tomb of Rachel, there came artillery fire. From Bethlehem itself came shells from heavier guns of the Egyptian army, set on the hill near the church built by the Crusaders over the birthplace of Christ. Tanks also moved in from the road itself and pushed on beyond to cut the road to Jerusalem. The Egyptians took the place, losing about 150 men in the taking.

The Israeli army, of which the long underground force, the Haganah was the backbone, came and retook it. For three bloody days they fought over that farm and its buildings. Three times it changed hands, but the last time found the Israelis in charge. The word "Haganah" means "defense." Its soldiers are among the best. They are now a part of the National army.

The day I saw it the settlement was yet a shambles. The main building, of stone and concrete, is a shell. About it the old trenches and sand-bagged gun positions are falling in. Its empty, battered rooms smell dankly of death and dampness. One could still pick up the corroded, empty brass shells of rifle ammunition fired in its defense. From its windows, some still sand-bagged, one could look down on the rows of barricades in the yards; concrete walls and trenches. On the opposite hill were the old Arab trenches. The place was a ruin.

But the settlement is again becoming a farm. The members are putting up new buildings. Already there are in the barns another 100 cows—all from America—bought by money supplied by American friends. There are new poultry houses going up.

Two of the committee members, both bowed and muscled by years of hard work such as only the Jewish farmers know who tackled one of the stony, eroded hills of Judea, looked on with pride and were not at all dismayed at the prospect of another start. They were Emanuel Bar-Hain (Son of Life) and Moshe Izkovitch, both of whom came from the ghettos of Poland to Palestine 28 years ago. They were from Polish farms and they have devoted their lives to building up this new country which now, as they move on from middle age into their last span of years, is what they long dreamed it to be—their own country. They feel they have helped make it so with their toil. And they have.

They are the best types of the collective farms. One finds in them the inevitable few intellectuals who have sought to make their work a sort of cathartic for their frustrations and neurosis in other lands. They work hard and argue mightily. But they still are pedants and still are fussily frustrated. The farm work brings them no peace.

I went back to see a farm settlement I had visited in 1946. It is called "Ma'aleh Hahamisha."

When I saw it in 1946 the rocky hill was still fighting back. The trees had been planted. There were small fields of grain. Poultry houses were going up.

This time I found it doubled in size. The trees are surprisingly large, all of them the fir and cypress pine. There was even a large flower garden.

But, there were scars, too. There had been heavy fighting about it. The walls of some of the buildings were marred by shell-fire holes. Many were pitted with rifle fire and mortar fragments. In a grove of cypress trees was a large machine gun emplacement, heavily sandbagged. Close by was a bomb shelter for the women and children. All about us were the wounds of war.

Here I met an American who had been there on my former visit. The war had embittered him against American Jews. He was one of the intellectuals who had come years before and by work and toil sought to rid himself of the complexes and the angers which the burden of race in America had sown in his mind. He was impatient with all about him. Ten years of work had not quenched any of the fires within him. He had fought bravely and well in the war. He had moments of gentleness and moments of tension when some were half afraid of him. He was not typical. Race still was a burden to him, as it was not any longer to thousands who had come from other lands.

It was a good place. Many more had died there, going on to join the souls of the five who had died to give it a name. All about us were the sounds of building and of work. It had expanded. It had been farm and fortress. Now it was farm again but would, if necessary, return to a fortress.

The people in the dining hall looked just the same. There are new young ones. There were those I had seen in 1946. Their hill is still tough, but green and productive. It is almost impossible to believe the barren, rocky hills can be conquered, and it is not easy. A good seven years are required to begin to break even. But the hills can be brought back to life by what are perhaps the finest examples of soil conservation in the world.

About 20 percent of the population of Israel are farmers. There are several hundred Jewish farmers in America, but here there are several thousand of them working at all sorts of farm jobs, doing literally all the work. Great rock walls testify to rocks picked up and pried out of the soil. Buildings, stone and concrete, all are evidence of their skill.

In 1946, I visited several such farms and slept and ate there. I noted the evening meal was about the same today—plenty of thick-sliced brown bread, bowls of plum or peach butter, margarine, raw carrots and tea. The big meal, with meat and vegetables, is at noon.

It is a great and complex experiment that is being tried here, and which gives all evidence of success. But the basis of it always will remain the farm and how well it can produce. It is odd, in a way, that the newest nation in the world on some of the oldest soil finds that it, too, must build on agriculture.

I left it wondering what it would look like when next I saw it, in the years ahead.

We drove on to Ein Karem.

Here, in this one-time Arab village, John the Baptist was born. It is not far from Jerusalem. It clings to one side of a Judean hill in the picturesque manner of such villages. The terraces are green. The slender and graceful cypress trees look almost like young dancers poised on point. The vineyards, in winter, are cut back and dark. The square-cut stone and mud houses of the poorer Arabs are gray-white. The stone buildings of the richer Arabs are tan and wine-colored, brown and sand-toned. All of them catch the sun and hold it.

It was an Arab village, one of the rich ones. Now it is Jewish. A large part of it is set apart as a youths' school, where young orphans, many left so by the Nazi murders, and others whose parents send them there for training as farmers and tradesmen, are educated. They are from many countries. But they all chatter in Hebrew, the linguistic bridge which is enabling peoples of more than 20 tongues to become one, and avoid thereby a modern Tower of Babel.

An old mosque stands there. It is now a school. Its foundations are ancient stones on which once stood a synagogue. Excavations have uncovered the site of an old city. It may have been the original city of Israel, old when John the Baptist was born here.

Boys worked in a carpenter shop, making toys. In another, boys worked making furniture. Girls were working in vegetable and flower gardens. Others, small ones of about 12, were carrying the repaired iron cots from a shop where older boys and supervisors worked. On a playground an older girl, a leader, taught dancing. It is too bad that institutions always have to have an air of "institutionalism." It is perhaps inevitable. This one was pleasant, well run and clean. The children looked happy and healthy.

In a sense it was a remarkable scene. There were children playing there from a dozen countries. None had been in Israel more than nine months.

"The children learn Hebrew rapidly," said a young Czech girl who showed me about. "The old persons who come cling to old ways. The young ones change old ideas for new as they learn to put on clean, fresh clothes."

I believe she is right. Everything I see of the young of Israel makes me believe it.

We visited some of the houses, now dormitories for the children. They were spotless. Women, most of them widows from Germany, Poland and Austria, were doing sewing and supervision tasks.

They spoke with horror of the dirt the Arabs had left behind them when they obeyed the Grand Mufti's voice on their radios and departed, sure of returning in two weeks when, as the Mufti said, the Jews would be driven into the sea.

In the village proper are families of Jews from Turkey, from Romania, from Jugoslavia and North Africa. Some are Sephardic Jews from Turkey who had lived there for more than 400 years since their expulsion from Spain by Ferdinand and Isabella.

The village, once an Arab city, is now a village of poor persons just entering into their new life. The two cafes had tea and bread, but no ready meals. They explained that not enough tourists come to their city save in summer to make it profitable to keep food ready.

We went to a Tnuva, a co-operative store supplied by products from co-operative farms. It was neat and clean and presided over by a stocky young Polish Jew. He helped us put two small tables together for four of us to eat. He sold us olives, soft cheese much like cottage cheese, bottles of sour "yogert," a clabber; sliced a large turnip for us, opened cans of sardines, sold us a loaf of flat bread, supplied knives and forks and looked on happily as we had a picnic lunch in his store.

Outside the door the life of the village went past us—children, men and women, some wearing bits of clothing from their countries of origin, high boots, peasant jackets, coats and caps.

A Jugoslav mother came in and bought bread. Her small son wanted candy, displayed in a case. She offered to buy a small, colored piece, but he broke into tears and howled miserably for a more expensive chocolate-covered bar. Children are alike the world over. I asked permission and bought it for him, thinking of a small boy about his size in America who also likes chocolate and who howls when he sees it and it is denied. His tears ceased and he thanked me with the chocolate already far in his mouth.

A heavily laden donkey went by. Over it all there was the sound of children at play, of conversation in the streets, the sea air, the spicy, acrid smell of the Middle East. It did not smell like an Arab village and there were refuse cans along the streets which the people used.

"Ein" means fountain or spring, and "Karem" means vineyard—Fountain of the Vineyard. Many of the names are picturesque.

One asks why the Arabs fled. They fled from new Jerusalem to the old. They fled from Tel Aviv and from Haifa, but not from Nazareth. Nor did they go from Abu Ghosh, a village near Jerusalem, or from several others.

The deserted villages have been occupied by new immigrants. There is no telling exactly why the Arabs departed. Their chief Moslem priests asked them to go. They never had much leadership. Most of them went. But many remained. They have fared well. They are full citizens. They serve in the army. They are seen in the shops and cafes of Jerusalem. Those who remained look satisfied and content. There is no discrimination against them. Their head men who told them to remain have gained great face. The Israeli Arab always had the highest standard of living in the Middle East. It is even more true today. But in the villages they left there are no signs remaining to say they were ever there.

There are about a half million Arabs living in displaced persons camps. Their fellow Arabs are doing little or nothing for them. They are resented by their Moslem brothers and by Christian brothers of Arab persuasion as well.

But they were not driven out.

It was their infamous Mufti (religious leader) who ordered local leaders in what was then Palestine, to lead guerrilla fighting from Arab villages as long as they could, and then withdraw with all their population.

It was the Mufti himself who talked daily on the Arab radio from Cairo urging this same procedure. The word was for all the Arabs to depart. There was no need for a peaceful Arab to leave.

The Jewish leaders in Haifa, for example, went in a body to the Arab leaders and earnestly besought them not to depart, but to remain.

The City of Nazareth today is an Arab town. Most of them are Christian Arabs. They occupy all their homes and their lands as before. They suffered no harm.

They are there simply because they did not go to war and were not interested in fighting on the side of Egypt, Syria, Transjordan, Lebanon and so on. They are citizens of Israel and enjoy all the rights of any other citizen.

The Druse villages are occupied, as always, by the Druses, who also did not choose to fight for foreign armies, but wanted peace. They, too, are prosperous.

Near Jerusalem, for example, is a large Arab town of Abou Ghosh. It always enjoyed peaceful relationships with its neighbors. It still does. It has representatives in the Government. Its people are citizens. Arabs from this town are seen in the cafes of Jerusalem, the business houses and in the movies. Its shiek says of the war, "We wanted peace. We had had no trouble with the Jews. They had been friends, not enemies. So, we knew what the radio and agents said was lies."

It is not at all unusual, in the distance of a half dozen miles, to find a deserted, blasted Arab village and a prosperous one. The only difference is that one went to war on the losing side and the other didn't. There are many Arabs left in Israel. In the Negeb the Bedouin tribes refused to follow the Mufti and remained. They enjoy all their rights, many of which date back to ancient days.

Of course there are thousands of Arabs in displaced persons camps. They are there because they were displaced by war, and not because they are Arabs, or because they were captured and

put there. They are free to come and go in those camps. Some
have applied for permission to come back to Israel and are there.
A commission is at work on a settlement of the property rights.
But it is simply not true to say they were heartlessly driven out
because the implication there is they were peaceful, innocent
folk greatly and unjustly put upon. The contrary is true. Their
own leadership and their own decision are responsible. The British
mandate was conditioned on regard for rights of the Arabs. The
inescapable facts are—publicly asserted up to about two months
before the British departure—that up to that time the Jewish
Agency was asking for, and was eager and willing to accept, a
bilateral government of Arabs and Jews. They were always eager
through the years to have such a government and it always was
withheld.

The tragedy of the Arab is his leadership, which has exploited
him as pitilessly as if he were slave. This is true even now.
Defeated in war, they despise their fellow Arabs whom they
called out of the country.

13

"*No Generality Is True*"

JERUSALEM—This is a city which proves the old axiom that "no generality is true, not even this one."

It is harsh, its critics say. But, when one in a moment of despondency has decided that to be true, the city becomes very lovely and gentle. If it is spring there may be the scent of almond blossoms on the evening air, or the wind may be blowing cleanly from the hills. The severe lines of the hills become soft in an afternoon's haze and moonlight in any city on or close to the Mediterranean always is lovely in the streets.

No generality is true—Jerusalem is herself.

There is the weight of history on her and there is in her the pressure of the future.

There is not much "to do" at night. There are a few restaurants and the occasional melody of a cafe piano. But, it is a quiet city.

The King David Hotel is changed. Four years ago it was one of the famous, legendary international hotels. The British command had headquarters there. The lobby was brilliant with uniforms at tea time and the cocktail hour was gay. The bar was crowded and the conversation was in French and English with a few cynical phrases in Yiddish from newspaper correspondents in the booths.

The staff was severely British in the offices. On the floors and in the elevators it was largely Egyptian and Arab . . . British trained and very, very efficient.

The Irgun terrorists blew up the British wing of it in the summer of 1946, killing and wounding Britons, Jews and Arabs. It was one of the major chapters in the inexorable march of events brought on by the British, who themselves tried terror but of course could not go all the way to totalitarian ruthlessness, and hence were defeated.

It is not possible morally to defend the terrorist actions. Yet, it is extremely unlikely there would have been a Jewish state without them. Nations born in violence, with their partisan terrorists enshrined as heroes, tend to shudder and condemn violence. The Jewish Agency likely would have been nullified in many respects but for the extremists. Now, they are become a part of the legend and are becoming integrated into history.

I found the King David staffed now by no glittering array of Egyptians and Arabs, but largely by drably clad women whose stories went deeply back into the tragedies of Europe. There were no uniforms. The untrained staff, men and women, slowly learning the myriad tasks of running a large hotel, fitted into this new Israel, where there was not enough of anything save courage, work and a dream.

The best night spot for newspaper men was the office of the Palestine Post, with its wounds of Arab terrorism still visible. A truck laden with a large amount of explosive, probably dynamite, was backed against the building one night and touched off, killing and wounding some of the staff.

One night we talked there until dawn. The folklore of war, which someone has called the patches of history, have not yet been collected. One hears stories of the underground activities, of the bringing in of illegal immigrants and stories of such romantic and fantastic impossibility that they seem incredible.

It was on this evening of talk and argument, I met one of the most extraordinary journalists I have ever encountered. He is very efficient and able and a very fine gentleman. He is crippled, one leg being quite a bit shorter than the other.

Yet he was in a partisan night attack on the Jaffa gate of the old city of Jerusalem. It was, at best, a quixotic, foolish charge with only the merest of chances. About 100 of them made the charge, men and a few women. Most of them were killed. One of them was a girl, by all accounts beautiful and fine. She was handling a tommygun in the charge and an Arab Legion bullet got her in the forehead. The charge was foredoomed to failure, since it was against experienced troops. It had as its purpose

the panicking of the Arab population in the old city. They felt
if they could take the gate and hold it, the population would
panic and the Arab Legion be unable to bring reserves to the
gate. It was badly planned in that the partisans themselves did
not have any reserves at all.

But as long as I live I will always remember that charge as
if I had seen it and this particular newspaperman making the
charge on his crippled leg.

Days later I was seated in the cocktail lounge of the Gat-Rimon
Hotel talking with some Israeli journalists when a young man
entered escorting a small, frail young lady. She looked very shy
and demure and tiny. They took a seat near us and I observed
to my companions that the young lady appeared so retiring and
naive it was really a shame to bring her into so materialistic a
place, even, as a cocktail bar.

Whereupon my companions broke into what is called loud
and merry laughter.

The demure young lady, they said, who must have weighed
no more than 99 pounds, was the severe partisan who was a bomb
expert in the days of the British mandate and who allegedly was
the one who had managed, working from France, to get one through
to Britain in one of the old Mosaic law killings. A British soldier
had been tried and acquitted for the particularly brutal murder
of a young boy in Palestine. Following the trial, he had been
sent out of the country. He was still believed guilty and was so
found by the underground organization to which the young lady
belonged. She it was, so they say, who managed to get a bomb
delivered in England to the brother of the British soldier. The
bomb did its job and the law of an eye for an eye and a tooth
for a tooth was upheld.

My demure young lady also had spent six months in a Belgian
jail, having been caught at the Belgian border with a bomb which
she was on her way to deliver to another person who had left
Palestine for the safety of England. Her mother had been killed
by the Nazis in France. She had helped out even then, at the
age of 12, in carrying messages and explosives.

I also was introduced one evening to a fine young woman
greatly taken up with her young son of a half dozen months.

She looked very maternal and, I am sure, was. I was only mildly surprised to discover, later on, that she had been one of the demolition experts of the underground and later of the Israeli Army and was considered its most daring.

Later on, at Fortress Iraq Suwedian I saw some of her work. That girl, whom I had seen caring for her child, had crawled through barbed wire, passed Egyptian sentries, fixed a terrific charge of explosives against the concrete wall, set the fuse going, and escaped without injury from the blast which breached the wall. She carried out many, many demolition jobs under extremely difficult conditions and at great risk.

For a long time here, almost every person was in effect an intelligence agent. The British were caught, like Gulliver, in the net of it. One of the puzzles which interests me most is the failure of the British mandate here. To the students of history it will become a subject to be examined in books and articles for years to come. The British went on from failure to failure here, caught in a web which they themselves had woven.

The original error was a preposterous one. They sent here, to govern the Arab and Jewish populations, men who were used to governing in the Sudan or in other backward "native" colonial regions. These men, used to dealing with an ignorant, more or less docile native type, might have done all right with the Arab population. But they simply did not know how to deal with the Jewish population, which was intelligent, intensely nationalistic, cultured and skilled.

Had the British set up a civil service system of self-government, similar to the one in India, there likely would be no Jewish State here today. There would likely be one with a dominion status in which a bilateral government of Arabs and Jews would be functioning. As late as six months before the proclamation of the Jewish State, the people here would have settled for such a bilateral government.

But the British went from error to error, pulling out to leave what they must have thought would be a state of chaos which, in turn, would require their coming back. It was then the really daring, wonderfully well-conceived, long-time plan of the Jewish organization paid off. The settlements were fighting outposts, just as our own in America were in the days of the Indian wars when our people were moving west and outlying farms about a stockade were outposts. The small defense organization, the Haganah, fought well. There was the will to fight. The invading armies were badly led and had no will for war. The nationalist spirit carried the people through to the new State and the British had made an error from which they could not at all recover.

The partisan deeds were many and help explain why the new State was possible. Violence has been a part of all great struggles for independence. They are ugly until the patina of years and history covers them.

14

In Which There is a Yemenite Boy

TEL AVIV, Israel—There is no city anywhere in the world quite like this one of Tel Aviv, thrusting its modern, balconied, stuccoed, concreted, plastered architecture up beside the Mediterranean and from among its many trees— tamarisk, eucalyptus, cypress and Australian pine.

Like the city, they are newly planted. In 1909 there was nothing here but sand dunes, stretching from the ancient city of Jaffa, which King Solomon knew. (This is the first thing a citizen tells a visitor and it has become almost a cliche which the sophisticated deplore. But it is true.) Today there is a city of 250,000 polyglot persons, each feeling, "This is my country."

Its streets by day are busy with an almost impossible traffic. By day its sidewalks swarm with people. There is a family in almost every room in this country and at night they go out on the streets and to cafes.

There is something of Vienna here. Many former cafe operators of the Austrian capital are here. There are literally hundreds of cafes, large and small, with their sidewalk chairs and tables.

The people are fascinating to watch. There is no racial type, no uniformity, no generalization to be made save the crowds appear young. One hears many languages. One sees all sorts of faces, but all—or almost all—have a look of belonging. One wonders what sort of culture will emerge here and what sort of person will come from the melting pot into which so much human material is being thrown.

There are touches of America. There are ice cream cones and peanuts. But the old man selling the peanuts along the streets and beside the movie houses also sells sunflower and melon seeds. There are signs of the East, Middle Europe and the West. But the old Palestinian aristocracy of 10 years ago already is sub-merged. This is a workers' country and it will become more so. It is semi-Socialist but, unless a world crisis in trade and com-merce comes, it will never become completely socialized. The spirit of enterprise is strong and will endure.

It is a city in a nation which works hard. America, which never managed to get the Palestine problem in perspective and cannot fix this new Israel (and the latter is difficult), must keep in mind it is a Jewish State. The cities, save for a few Arabic ones, are Jewish. The policemen, the house painters, bricklayers, steel workers, metal workers, plasterers, carpenters, the soldiers, the aviators, waitresses, waiters, mechanics, common laborers, all are Jews.

There has never been a story quite like this in all the history of the world. I do not pretend to know all about it. It is so vast a human experiment in economics, humanity and government that one cannot digest it easily or soon. But it is a yeast working unceasingly in the Middle East and thereby in the loaf of which all of us eventually must eat.

Tel Aviv is now, its people say. Jerusalem is of the past and Haifa of the future. Crowded, busy, in a hurry, it is noisy yet vital. Both Jerusalem and Haifa look down their noses at it. "Tel Aviv is not Israel," they say. But in a sense it is even more the story of Israel than either of its rivals.

In the United States I have had people ask me, "What in the world goes on over there in Israel, anyhow?" Now that I am here I wish I could answer. It is an experiment so daring, so complex, so seemingly impossible that one is staggered by the physical facts of it.

Let's set down a few.

Since May, 1948, more than 370,000 immigrants have come to this tiny, new country, risen from the dead of nations after 2,000 years.

The total population of the country is now a little more than 1,000,000. So, from the figures one may see that more than a third of the entire population has been here less than two years.

They have come from many countries, speaking many lan-guages. There have come here some of the finest minds in the world, some of its best artists, musicians, intellectuals, thinkers, teachers and philosophers. There have come, too, degraded and retarded peoples from the ghettos of fearful and retarded Eastern countries. Some did not know how to sleep on beds; had never seen a toothbrush; did not know the meaning of toilets, sanitation, or education. They came from the crowded corners of ancient Eastern cities where for generations their lives had been those of a struggle for survival.

The Yemenites, for example, came from isolated, backward, ignorant and feudal Yemen. There was no wandering in the wilderness for them. They were flown in over the Red Sea. Yemen ordered them out when the fighting halted with Yemen one of the defeated Arab nations. Deeply religious, nut brown in color, they came with their ignorance, superstitions and fears. They were afraid of doctors. Their women hid in corners of tents to have babies rather than go to a hospital. They put their bundles on the cots and slept on the floor.

Their women, when forced to go to the hospital, refused to be examined by male doctors. They fought screaming against nurses who took their sick babies from them for treatment.

Yet, after a few months, the ferment is stirring. They are learning. The old women, illiterate, and without any status, are demanding of their men they be allowed to learn to read. They are taking rights never dreamed of in medieval Yemen. Some of the men are cutting off their four ritualistic curls.

On the Jewish Sabbath we were driving to Haifa. Along the road we saw a Yemenite boy and stopped to give him a ride. Joe Davis, soldier and friend, questioned him. The boy was bright and impish in appearance. His brown eyes were merry and unafraid as they looked out of his small face, and he sat joyfully in the fast car. He said he was 12 years old. He had been in Israel four months.

"I thought you Yemenites were religious," said Joe Davis, accusingly, and speaking in Hebrew. "What are you doing out here on the road?"

"I am religious," he said. "I have prayed already." He knew what was behind the questions.

"What if your father catches you riding in a car on the Shabbus?" (Sabbath.)

"If he catches me I will be whipped," said the boy, grinning, "so I will manage not to be caught."

"Do your parents speak Hebrew?"

"No, only I." (This was said proudly, and with reason. He had learned it in four months. It is amazing how children pick up languages.)

"What have you done with your curls? I thought Yemenites wore them."

"I cut mine off. I didn't like them any more."

"How do you like to ride in a motor car?"

"I like it very much. It is the ninth time in my life I ride in one. In all my life I had not ridden in one until I came here. In Yemen, Jews are not permitted to ride in cars."

"Would you like to go back to Yemen?"

"Not I. Here it is much better."

We let him out at a crossroad near his new village and he sped away up it, uncaught. For that boy the old walls had dropped, and the horizons opened up before him with the endless vistas every boy of every race ought to be able to see. Not all ghettos are in European cities. There are thousands like him here, seeing those vistas in terms of a new life and a new country. It is little wonder that one finds here a nationalism which at times is disturbing, but which always is understandable.

Let us return to the dry statistics which sometimes are necessary. Here is how they have come to this country since May, 1948, in approximate numbers, which do not include the many refugees who came from China, from Latin America and the Scandinavian countries.

Poland sent about 90,000, mostly DPs.

Romania sent some 40,000, about half DPs.

Bulgaria has 36,000 here, the only European war country where there was no anti-Jewish campaign.

There are 20,000 here from Czechoslovakia.

Germany and Austria are represented by 12,000.

Yugoslavia has 8,000 immigrants here.

But Turkey has sent an amazing 30,000 persons.

There are 40,000 here from North Africa, Tripolitania, Tunis,

Algiers and Morocco.

Tiny Yemen has sent 40,000. These people migrated to Yemen in 586 B. C. after the destruction of the Temple. They believed they were doomed to mourn forever for Zion because they rejected the invitation of the prophet Ezra to return. When this present invitation came, thousands of them walked as much as 40 miles across desert country, leaving all behind them, to take the "magic carpet" airplane to the land their ancestors had left 2,000 years ago.

Egypt has 15,000 Jews here. There are 3,000 from India, about the same number from France, from Belgium and Holland.

There is almost no country that is not represented here.

Keep in mind that of a population of a little more than 1,000,000, more than 370,000 have come since May, 1948.

They continue to come, every week, almost every day.

Before the great exodus from Europe and Africa it was possible to give some indoctrination to those preparing to go to Palestine. They arrived prepared for the physical and mental problems they encountered.

For more than two years that has not been possible. They have come in such vast numbers and in so short a time, it has not been possible to prepare them.

Oriental, Arab-like, they have come from Yemen, North Africa and Iraq until they outnumber the "old settlers."

It is fascinating, looking on the polyglot crowds, hearing the many tongues, to speculate on what culture will develop and on what the Israeli of the future will be like.

In the Cafe Hesse in Jerusalem, I talked of this with Gershon Agron, editor of the influential English-language Palestine Post. He is an ex-copy reader from the Philadelphia Bulletin who came here more than 20 years ago. He now is Minister of Information in the new Government. He also is a legend in the Middle East, shrewd, smart, informed, courageous.

"There are four strata in Israel," he said. "There are the young ones who were born here and who fought in the war. They are called 'Salra' from the cactus plant of that name and are the children of persons who came here from other countries. During 'the war' they flew planes, fought in the infantry and in partisan raids. Before that they were among the resistance groups opposing the mandate government. They grew up with Hebrew as their language. They have never questioned their belonging. This land is theirs. They have a dream about it. It is they who will be the core about which the culture of the future will grow.

"We have, too, the intellectuals from foreign lands, the scholars, teachers and professionals. They learn Hebrew, but they cling to their old languages, German, English or French. There is next the immigrant groups and the DPs. There is fourthly the remnant of medievalism and the Orient, including both their ignorant ones and their scholars. These are Yemenites, Persians, Kurds and Algerians.

"The first three classes will fuse in the years ahead, and they will create the new type, the new culture. The children of the latter will develop with the first three. Schools modernize minds."

There is here a religious problem, as there inevitably had to be. The orthodox and the religious scholars, who sit all day studying the Talmud, annually have less influence. They are strongest in Jerusalem where most of them are congregated. Their influence is least in Haifa. But, in both Tel Aviv and Jerusalem they have managed thus far to prevent buses running during the daylight hours of the Sabbath. Tel Aviv, and perhaps the entire nation, is soon to break away from that because of the shortage of personal transport and because only the private car owner can move about. Social demands break down religious strictures. In America, Sunday movies came and baseball, because the average person, with no car and no recreation, demanded it and had a right to it. It is the same here. There will not be a religious state set up here. It will always have a deeply religious core, but the strict orthodoxy is disappearing as surely as the bearded, skull-capped, patriarchal rabbis and the calf-like ones with the traditional four long curls, from the small, self-imposed ghettos of Jerusalem.

"The future will take care of that," say leaders, as they watch the young immigrants, but a few weeks in the country, cut off their curls and adopt modern ways.

15

An Army of Fighters

Tᴇʟ Aᴠɪᴠ, Israel—How good is the Israeli army?

I'd say it already is—or is well on the way to becoming—the best, very small army in the Middle East.

There is censorship about the military. That is not surprising. The Arabs are rearming. They have the man power and they possess more arms.

But in the recent war the Israeli army won. At some points there was bloody stalemate, but the net was a surprising victory. At the beginning of the war they had three field guns—just three. They used to fire them in an afternoon and that night pull them to another region to fire the next morning. They obtained some arms during the war. But they never had enough.

They won it on intelligence, leadership and a hard core of fanatic courage.

The army that won was a partisan army, built under the eyes of the British who held the mandate.

Now, how good is the modern army? I have just concluded a visit to a training camp for recruits. I talked there with an impressive Lt. Col. Mordecai Aksamite, Camp Commander.

"All you see here you can write and all I tell you may be printed," he said. "This is a camp for recruits. It is no secret we are training men."

What I saw astonished me. Here, on a large parade ground, were men being trained in the rudiments of drill. Drill instructors, tough and as harsh of voice as those of the United States Marines at Cherry Point or Parris Island, were putting them through the drill. I have never seen men drilled harder or more thoroughly in my life. They march as did the British, with the right arm swung high and freely. The DIs were making them stamp and pound on the turns. It was sharp and very, very businesslike. It would have delighted the heart of any military man.

The Israeli soldiers wear the British-type uniform, with certain modifications. The men are smartly dressed and well equipped. The uniforms are made in Israel. The boots come from Israel and Australia. The caps, shirts and khaki pants are from America.

The training camp routine is hard, the discipline severe. Yet so intense is the Israeli spirit that few men fall victim to it.

The men work hard. Their day is nine hours. Two or three nights each week there are night drills. They are fed well and housed well, although American soldiers would not think well of the Israeli bed. It is a good mattress laid on a plank base. There are plenty of blankets and sheets.

The men in training are given physical training in calisthenics and over very tough obstacle courses. Included in these latter are those over which live ammunition is fired, as is customary in all army training today.

A small but complete army, including aviation troops, is being trained.

Recruits may be either volunteers or selective service. At 18 each Israeli youth must serve two years. Many volunteer for the regular army. They may volunteer for three, four or five years.

The training period, of a varying number of weeks, is done in two divisions. The native-born Israeli train in one group. Because so many thousands have come to Israel from so many nations, and speak so many tongues and are, often, in inferior physical condition, they are trained separately. For these latter ones there are, in addition to the hours of drill and instruction, extra hours of schooling in Hebrew, the national language.

By the time they learn their rifle they must also learn enough Hebrew to get along. They do it. They also fill out enormously. Some of the Yemenites, whose generations of malnutrition and bad health have produced a slender, rather frail youth with almost no shoulders, gain two and three inches in the chest and put on 20 and even 30 pounds of weight. They are enormously proud of their new muscle and dimensions. Almost all the immigrant recruits gain from 10 to 15 pounds.

Once the period of training is done all are mixed together and sent to permanent units. There isn't any doubt about this much— once an Israeli soldier has come through the training course he is a good soldier, as well trained as any in any other country.

Most of those with any rank are combat veterans. There are few Jewish young men who did not experience combat in the recent war against the Arab states. There is in this army a fine core of experience. Its morale is high.

It is a literate army. It reads books, goes to concerts and has, too, a sense of humor. It knows why it is being trained, why Israel must have an army, and it expresses itself in a banner hung over one of the barracks doors:

"We Train for Peace, But We Prepare for War."

The men who are its officers include many who served for some years with the British army and with the Jewish Brigade in that army. That war was bitterly and fanatically fought. The Jewish army won because it had better leadership, was more intelligent and wanted to fight for the land and the people.

It will fight again if it has to do so. If it does it will fight well. How good is it?

I don't know. But I believe it to be very, very good indeed.

After we had had a look at the Israeli army training camp, we went into the small club for officers.

There, sitting about a table on which were tea and cakes, we talked about wars and armies. It so happened that of the half dozen officers present, from the Colonel commanding on down, every one had served at some time in the British army.

The drill I had seen had been British. I asked Col. Mordecai Aksamite, commanding, how much of it was British.

"The basis," he said, "because it is not a bad system and also it is what we know best. But it is by no means all British. We have borrowed from the Americans and the French. Also, we have made our own Israeli discoveries and applied them so as to care for our terrain and specific problems."

"What is American?" I asked.

"The bayonet practice," he said. "The British methods are for mass use and are cold. Bayonet fighting is hot and man to man. When a soldier comes to use a bayonet he is hot and he is after one particular man. The American method more nearly suits our personality. So we have adopted it entirely."

One hears here many stories about the stupidity of the British rule. I had seen some of it here four years ago.

"Colonel," I said, "what was wrong with the British methods from your viewpoint?"

"Well," he said, "we wanted our country and they didn't want us to have it. That is the basic thing which was wrong. But I know what you mean. It was that in dealing with Colonials the British always made them feel a second-rate man. I was 10 years in the British army. I was in a Commando group of Palestinians in the last war. But because I was from Palestine I was not paid as much as British soldiers of the same rank. Our mess was not the same. I could not live on my major's pay. A British major could. It was so of all Colonials, the Indians, Ceylonese and so on. That did not make me happy. Once, in the desert with this Commando unit, my men needed boots. Those they had were worn out. I went to the supply office. It meant nothing to him, but when I asked him for an issue of boots for my men he sneered and said, 'Don't tell me that Palestinians who go about barefooted all the time need boots to wear.' In hundreds of little ways they sought to make a man feel inferior. I do not hate the British. I never did. I have many British friends and individually they are fine people. But here they were lost from the moment they tried to use terror and force against a people who believed themselves morally right and who were weary of years of being treated as secondary citizens."

The story of British rule here is one of the tragic puzzles of history. The time came when, with thousands of soldiers, several thousands of police and agents, they were helpless in the face of a people determined to be free. The British also worked their way into such a position that even when the terrorists began to retaliate against them they were helpless to fight back and were made to deliver themselves into the hands of the terrorists. The British began to flog captives. When the terrorists flogged a British officer the British ceased flogging. The British hanged some terrorists, or men accused of it. The terrorists hanged two British soldiers. The British quit hanging terrorists. The terrorists knew they had won.

The time came, as near as one can figure it out from all the stories told, when almost every Palestinian was a volunteer agent against the British and an active participant with the resistance movement. One of the prize stories concerns two men who were greatly trusted by the British as Palestinian informers. These men were protected, often elaborately. They were transported in armored cars when they had to be taken through dangerous parts of the city. These informers were present at British parties and talked loudly against the Jews and fawned on the Arab notables present.

It was they—with orders—who kept urging the British to pull out. Their line was that once the British pulled out the Jewish terrorist organizations would fight each other and the Arab armies would be able to walk in, making it necessary for the British to come back and take over to restore order.

Whatever the reason, and of course there were many other pressures, the British did depart.

The Jewish population, which had looked forward eagerly to killing the two notorious informers, was literally dumfounded and agape to see the two marching in the front ranks of one of the most active terrorist organizations. They had been members all the while and had fed information to it.

British actions in the days before they pulled out left many bitter wounds which will not heal for a long, long time.

Arab terrorists and the Arab Legion were unofficially aided against the Jewish fighters. Beside one ruined building on the Jerusalem road out of Tel Aviv there is a memorial to seven men who, defending the building, were disarmed by the British. An hour later their throats were cut by Arab soldiers. The British had acted to "keep order along the road."

These stories persist. Relations continue to improve with the British. The Middle East must have peace and Britain wants it to have peace. But there can be no peace without participation by Israel. Jordan is eager to make peace because Jordan is almost bankrupt. Peace, not war, should come. But old wounds give Israel the will and the courage to build and endure and sacrifice.

16

A Small Girl Remembers

T EL AVIV, Israel—About 55 years ago a small girl, about three and a half years old, watched in half-understanding fear while her father piled the furniture against the door of their small house in Kiev, Russia. She did not quite know what her parents meant when they whispered about a pogrom, but she knew fear. It was the first thing she remembered.

Later on she came to America with her immigrant parents. They settled in Milwaukee. There she went to school, graduated, worked in the public library, taught school.

In 1921 she came to Palestine, remembering that night when she was not yet four and the furniture against the door. She wanted to work for a country to which the oppressed might come and have a home. She entered a settlement farm and did the hard, grinding work of it.

Today that child, teacher, dreamer and worker has become Golda Meyerson, Minister of Labor of Israel, the country which her fear, her dream, her sweat and her mind helped create.

About the same number of years ago also in Russia, a young boy picked up dreams from listening to his elders talk about a country where they could have a home free from fear of violence and discriminations.

Today that boy is David Hacohen, Deputy Mayor of Haifa, Israel's beautiful seaport city, and one of the political and industrial leaders of the new country. I also think he is one of the great, deeply honest, sincere men I have met, as I believe Golda Meyerson to be one of the great women of her time.

They, as Minister of Labor and a power in the majority political party, Mapai, have heaviest upon them the problem of this new, dramatic, feverish and expanding new country—Israel. There are similar stories of all those who have striven here as pioneers.

Its population has increased by more than 370,000 persons— immigrants from more than 20 countries speaking as many languages—in less than two years. Its total population is little more than 1,000,000. The history of Israel is a history of immigration.

Immigration continues at the rate of about 12,000 per month. Plans were ready to take about 90,000 this year—1950. A budget was being strained to meet it.

Then came the news. Iraq notified Israel she would permit all her Jewish residents who wished to migrate to Israel to do so— and that of the approximate 150,000 such at least 70,000 to 100,000 wanted to come.

That meant that instead of 90,000 new citizens this year Israel will receive possibly, and without doubt, about 160,000, probably more. It could go to 250,000. And may.

It is easy to figure what that does to a budget.

Israel is building housing fast. In the last six months of 1949 she built 30,000 houses, most of them small. She has planned 50,000 for 1950.

That looked like a good dent in the need. But, with at least 160,000 new persons coming—not 70,000—the housing plan for 1950 now seems pitifully small. Before the news from Iraq the nation needed 70,000 rooms and had 50,000 blue-printed and budgeted. Last year was a terrific year. A total of 247,000 new immigrants arrived in that year. They are coming by the thousands every month.

That creates a camp problem. There are 19 immigrant camps where the many persons from many lands are received, medically examined, and housed in barracks and tents. There are today 84,000 persons in such camps. The conditions are not all desirable. The people are fed enough and they are gaining in weight and health. Infant mortality is far below what it was in their respective homes. Education of the young and instruction for the adults, is carried on. Yet, the authorities frankly admit the time immigrants must remain in camp is too long. It averages about five to six months. As fast as homes are provided they are moved out. But the intake is faster than the outgo. And the immigrants are coming.

"Our two great headaches are houses and jobs," says Golda Meyerson. "The camps breed discontent and discouragement, especially among the less informed and those who are so illiterate they are unable to understand well what is told them. But, once out they fit in well. Thank God we have had enough medical supervision to keep down illness and epidemics—although we live with worry.

"We need investments here and such investments will make money, if well planned. The government will make concessions to any businessman. Americans are about the only ones who can do this. Their currency is not blocked. Those in European countries who are willing cannot take their money out to invest elsewhere.

"Sometimes," she sighed, "I think American businessmen don't understand what foreign exchange means. They don't have to understand. But, they can't understand that today—the entire world is dependent on having not a franc, a lire, or a pound, but a dollar. We had one builder who came to us and wanted to build houses. We said to him here is the land. It is yours. What else do you want? He told us and we gave him that. Then he wanted us to pay him $25,000,000 in cash to build them and pay him in dollars." She smiled wryly. "If we had the $25,000,000," she said, "we would build them ourselves. We want people to invest their money here and make a profit, and not wish to take it all out in dollars every month."

Israel carried her own operations budget of 46,000,000 pounds, with the pound at $2.80. It is well over $100,000,000. The United Jewish Appeal last year sent a magnificent $55,000,000, or about 20,000,000 pounds. The government also has a large public works development budget of about 60,000,000 pounds. United Jewish Appeal aid is vital, but it must be noted that Israel is carrying her part of the load.

They all keep moving ahead. There is no thought of stopping immigration. The country was founded to take those who wanted a homeland. So, they will go on. The costs are great. An army must be built. Defense must be created.

And always, as the new houses are built, the new ones come

to the camps. There are always hands wanting work and families
wanting homes.

It is an incredible, complex problem and only a people such
as these, tired, but determined to carry on, could do it.

I believe they will.

Israel's war for independence, and the subsequent necessity
to arm and fight a small cold war of her own, brought increasing
austerity to the people. Nothing reflects it more than the facial
contortions of a gourmet at dinner on meatless days. There are
four meatless days each week, not one. No meat. No fowl. Fish
is permitted.

The fish, unfortunately, are not plentiful. In the first place
the nation had no trawlers to start with. It has some and is
getting more. The fish come in small lots fresh from the Mediterranean and the Sea of Galilee, and frozen from the Scandinavian countries.

Only in the small cafes do they know how to cook it. The
larger dining rooms seem to have given up with austerity and
they serve forth some very awful dinners, the waiters sad of face
and apologetic. The fish doesn't look cooked. It looks dead.
And the price is up in the big chips.

But, over in Jaffa, which is the one-time Arab part of Tel Aviv,
some new friends took us to an aromatic restaurant where the
same type fish, dipped in butter and fried, was served with
pickled peppers and cabbage and was excellent.

Prices are high. A movie costs 40 piasters, which is about
$1.10. Local cigarettes come about 50 cents the pack, American
brands about $1. Shoes, taxis, suits and food are above U. S.
prices. All eggs, meat, butter, milk and most perishable food
stuffs are strictly rationed. The Israeli citizen gets four eggs
per week. There is no cheating.

The population of more than a million is terribly crowded at
home and on the buses. Transportation is short. The distances
are such that taxis ply between Jerusalem and Tel Aviv, Haifa
and Tel Aviv, at good stiff prices, but people pay it to escape
the buses.

Income taxes are roughly equivalent to those in the United
Kingdom. But there is no black market worth the name and

austerity is shared alike, even by the tourists.

But, the people are taking it as well as the British did, and are, and with the usual number of complaints. The jokes are good and indicate the high morale.

One of them has an Israeli citizen paying his taxes and looking at his empty pocketbook, saying, mournfully:

"We waited 2,000 years for a Jewish state and it had to happen to me."

The crowded condition of the buses is best illustrated by the favorite cafe joke on the subject. On a very crowded bus a young man, unable to reach a strap, was holding onto the long beard of an old man standing next to him. At last the old man, weary of it, said severely indeed:

"Young man, let go my beard!"

"What," said the young man, "don't tell me you are getting off already?"

The cost of living and the rationing produce many stories. Dov Joseph, Minister of Supply, and Eleazer Kaplan, Minister of Finance, figure in most of them. The best one has to do with the day of a great army parade and holiday festival. The two ministers are flying in a plane looking down at the festive crowd.

"Look at them," said the minister in charge of rationing. "Did you ever see such happy people. If I could only throw some steaks down to them they would reach the very acme of happiness." The minister of taxation said, "No, if I could throw them down some dollars they would attain the peak of happiness."

The pilot turned and said, "You are both wrong. If I could throw both of you down, the people would be really happy." (This joke, in similar form, is told in the United States with President Truman as its principal.)

Dov Joseph is making a collection of the jokes and takes a great pride in the really good ones in which he figures.

Israeli is a dedicated country. It had to be successful to fight the British mandate government and then to wage a costly war with the Arab nations. There was not much time for fun. There is very, very little night life save that of the cafes, to which the people go to escape their crowded rooms. Night life consists chiefly of drinking of tea, beer or wine and talking. There are a few small cabarets.

There is one joke going the rounds of these clubs. The master of ceremonies announces that a friend of his has started reading anti-Semitic papers. When asked why, the friend replied, "Well, here all is austerity. We do not have enough to eat. The taxes are high. The cost of living is great. There are many sacrifices. Life is monotonous. The papers urge one to do without and to work harder lest we starve and die. The papers warn us there may be another war. So, I read the anti-Semitic papers. And what are they saying? They are saying the Jews have all the money and are going to rule the world." This is always good for a loud laugh.

All this means the spirit of the people is high. If peace will only come to the Middle East, and the beginning of it looks near, then Israel will emerge from austerity. She wants to buy and she has some goods to sell, although her domestic consumption is so thorough most of what she can make, at high costs, is used locally. Her high wages and small factory output will make it difficult for her to compete in many items on a world market. But, peace, with trade across the borders, will greatly relieve the present situation in which Israel, lacking dollars, is tightening her belt and doing without. Her money, which is inflated, is backed chiefly by a printing press and a dream—but it is sound.

There are more and more acres going into crops each year and within another two or three years the new nation should be producing about half her foodstuff needs. She now does about 40 percent of it.

Meanwhile, with a war to pay for and a possible second one to prepare for, austerity rules . . . and so tight are the borders there is almost no black market. It's austere, really, austere.

17

Where the Jordan Flows

METULAH—Last night I walked out on the balcony of my room in the small rural inn here called, in Hebrew, "The Inn of the Cypresses," and looked down into the deep Huleh Valley below where the river Jordan was receiving small tributaries and moving on toward the first of its three lakes.

Along the slopes I could see the twinkling lights of five kibbutzim, or communal farm settlements.

One of them was Mayan Baruch. I had visited it the afternoon before to see Evelyn Elkon and her brother, Hershel Elkon, one-time newspaper copy boy in Atlanta and once an employee of Rich's department store.

Evelyn Elkon graduated from Girls High in Atlanta and attended Agnes Scott College for two years. She and her brother both were active in Zionist work in Atlanta as were their parents. The latter now have come here and live in Haifa. They are Mr. and Mrs. Sam Elkon. They formerly had a grocery store in Atlanta.

Evelyn and her brother came to Israel in 1946 and were sent to the newly formed farm settlement of Mayan Baruch. It is located far in the north, in the region where was the old tribe of Dan. It was just being opened up and needed workers.

That meant they were put down in tents on the mountain slope near a valley. With their own hands they built their buildings. With their own hands they cleared the land of rocks and broke it to the plow. Today, after four years, it still is raw, but greatly progressed with comfortable, small buildings. It has large vegetable gardens. The day I was there they were shipping 100 crates of broccoli to the co-operative marketing quarters. Not all their land is yet in cultivation because they have only about 100 persons on the place, and need more. The work is divided. There must be cooks, cleaners, sewers, workers in the nursery where the children are kept all day; guards, blacksmiths, a bookkeeper and so on.

About a third of the population of such a settlement works on the land. Others do work which is closely associated, such as caring for cattle, sheep, goats, driving trucks, and so on. For example, I found Evelyn Elkon at her small apartment in one of the one-story, barracks-like buildings. She is married to a young man from Los Angeles, Ralph Bauman. They have a son 5½ months old, called Gidon. When she came she worked in the fields with the others. Now that she has a child she does not do field work, but is assigned to jobs which might be roughly defined as community housekeeping tasks.

I asked where the brother might be found and she told me he was one of those in charge of a large herd of sheep. They are kept for their milk, which is sent to a near-by co-operative cheese plant, where it is made into a really excellent white cheese which tastes something like Cheddar or the Greek Fetta. It is mildly like Roquefort, which, too, is made from sheep's milk.

"I'll bet some of my friends in Atlanta get a kick out of hearing I am a sheep herder," said Herschel, whom we found at the sheep barn. He helps care for the sheep and also is responsible for the carefully kept records of milk production, lambs, the feed and so on.

The kibbutz also has some milk cows, Holsteins, and their milk goes to the co-operative as well, for cheese and butter and for sale as fluid milk, the co-operative determining the division. This, plus their extensive vegetable farming, constitutes the farm's activities.

The two Atlantans have fitted in well. It is not always easy for Americans, used to a certain standard of living and to recreation, to submerge themselves in communal work on lonely and isolated farms. Evelyn and her brother have done it. They have carried their load. They are enthusiastic about it and they feel they have helped toward building a new country.

Both are proficient in Hebrew which is, of course, the national language. With so many persons coming from so many different lands it was necessary, beyond the historical reason, to have a common language. They have the typical settlement spirit, a belief in their own kibbutz and a desire to make it comfortable and more efficient.

I asked Evelyn Elkon, who seemed to be about 23, how she had made the transition.

"I knew about what to expect," she said. "I had been interested for a long time. I knew the work would have to be hard and I was ready. I did not approach it in just an idealistic manner. Some come full of idealism but can't take the work and the rough beginnings, when things are so primitive. Others become lonely and go. But most of us remain."

There was severe fighting all through the area where their settlement is located. The Syrian army came close by. Their kibbutz was not damaged, but they remained in a state of preparedness, with arms ready at all times.

"It is a little odd, your turning up here," Evelyn said. "Just a few nights ago I tuned in the radio and there was a man speaking. I said it sounded like your voice—I had heard you talk in Atlanta—and sure enough it was. You were doing a broadcast on The Voice of America program."

I wanted to ask some questions. I wanted to say, "Look, tell me about this. Are you sorry? Do you ever wish you hadn't come? Do you wish to chuck it now and go back home?"

I wanted to ask these questions, but I didn't. Certainly she had experienced moments of homesickness and doubt. But, the answer was before me.

(When I came back one of her teachers came to see me. "Tell me about Evelyn," she said, "I am so distressed about her. She was such a talented girl. Her parents sacrificed a great deal for her. She had genuine ability in arts. I can't imagine her working in a field or buried off in some isolated farm. Was she really happy? Does she want to stay?" I could answer her only that she was there and that she had found her place. She had been there long enough to know. I could not say that to the visitor who really goes and sees there is a sort of inner strength obtained from the experience. If I had said so I could not have explained it.)

There are many who do not care for farming. There are changes on the farms. On some there is a trend away from the nurseries and the communal dining rooms to more of a private, family life. Most of the newcomers who go to farming want their own piece of land.

We went on from Mayan Baruch to the small town of Metulah. It is one of the older settlements. It is at a point where the Lebanon border is almost in its front yard and the Syrian line not much further away. It is one of the first Jewish farm settlements in this country, and its farmers have fared well. Because it was, and is, a frontier town, the farmhouses were closely arranged, almost like a stockade. From my hotel room I can look down on lambs, sheep, chickens and turkeys, and it is well that the air here is so keen and crisp and fragrant that none sleeps late. At 6 o'clock this morning the lambs were "baaing," the turkeys gobbling, the roosters crowing, the hens cackling and a pet black lamb had even got into one of the downstairs hallways and was baaing there. Sleep ends with the dawn.

The scenery is magnificent. Across the way are the Lebanese mountains, snow-capped. All about the mountains rise and from my window I can see the road fork, one branch going to Sidon, the other to Damascus. Since the war with the Arabs, both roads are closed and the fields about them reportedly mined.

This is well above the ancient site of the tribe and city of Dan, from which came the phrase, "From Dan to Beersheba."

Not far from there the River Jordan wells out of a rock-strewn cave at the base of eternally snow-capped Mount Hermon, a short distance from the wretched hovels of an Arab town which stands where once stood the great city of Caesarea Philippi.

There is a brooding stillness about the place. It is fitting this should be so. It was on Hermon's heights that Jesus was transfigured before the three disciples, Peter, James and John. Jesus and the disciples could look down and see the beginning of the Jordan. It was this stream they followed to the lonely, eternal heights of Calvary.

There is something of the Jordan in the heart of every Christian. In small, rural churches, themselves lonely in isolation of hills and fields, congregations drink of the spiritual waters of the

Jordan. In rich city churches and in the shabby tents of curious sects dotting vacant lots on the edges of many towns, they sing of the Jordan and thirst for its symbolic waters.

It is equally significant to the Jews. The word Hebrew means "from across the river." In the misty dawn of recorded history the word Hebrew was applied to those stubborn shepherds who came from "across the river" into Palestine. It has been a part of their lives ever since.

It is not a large river. Its name means "descender." This is because its life is a descent, with a few pauses, to the confining reaches of the Dead Sea. Its source gushes from the cave and, joining others, cascades down toward the swampy, papyrus-filled marshes about Lake Huleh. The Huleh Valley is rich and green. The mountains about it, stark and beautiful by day with the austerity of their revealed stones and awesome evidences of centuries of erosion, are soft and serene in the haze of approaching dusk. Twilights in the quiet places of the Holy Land have in them an almost tangible spiritual quality of prayer and reflective withdrawal from material things.

In the valley are new farm villages springing up where no plow has been for ages. These are the settlements of Jewish farmers. Some have been farmers all their lives. Others are newly made agriculturists, taught by experts. There are more than 200,000 Jews on farms or in agricultural work and teaching. They begin with the land only. With their own hands, they build their farm and residential buildings. Some may be the collective-type settlements. Others may be the small-holders' farms where the homes are in a village but where each family has 10 or 12 acres of land.

Much of the swamp land about Lake Huleh, which lies deeply bordered by the green papyrus, is being drained and the rich muckland opened for vegetable farming.

Lake Huleh is the first of the Jordan's lakes. Here the river pauses after its first swift descent. The lake was called in Biblical times "The Waters of Merom."

Here (Joshua 4:11) the great Hebrew leader and general fought and defeated the kings of the north. These kings met beside the lake and formed their plans and it was here that

Joshua and his army fell upon them, as directed by the Lord, and drove them into flight with great attendant slaughter.

The young river disappears into the swamps and the lake and seems to rest there for a while. When it emerges, the descent is swifter even than before. It is but 11 miles to the Sea of Galilee. In those 11 miles, the river falls an astounding 682 feet.

That great lake, or sea, called also after the cruel and decadent emperor, Tiberias, lies in the area Christ liked best. It was in Galilee he performed most of his miracles and spent much of his adult life. Today there are ancient ruins about the rim of the lake, or sea, where once were the gentile Greek trading cities. The city of Tiberias is small but charming in relatively modern antiquity. There are cemented terraces there, and one may sit by the lake and have lunch or dinner. Young boys dive off the terraces for swims, and gulls fly about seeking crumbs. Fishing boats always may be seen upon the water. It is not a true sea. It is about 12 miles by 7½ at its most expansive point. It is shaped like a great heart. Hills surround it. On one of them was preached the Sermon on the Mount. By one of them the miracle of the loaves and fishes took place.

The Jordan pushes on out of the sea without much pause. It has built up a rich delta through the myriad of years it has flowed there. The flow is sure but slowed down by the flat of the delta. Here and there willows and eucalyptus trees dip their branches into it. The banks are grassy.

Not far from the Sea of Galilee, along the valley road south, there is a new park. It is a small one. Flowers bloom riotously in it. Shrubs apparently enjoy growing there. In the middle of the park is a squat, ugly, sinister tank. It marks the farthest advance of the Lebanon and Syrian armies into Jordan Valley. The tank was Syrian. It was disabled and its crew made captive. Now the beauty of nature competes with its brutal ugliness.

Here the river, which began 600 feet above sea level, is 680 feet below the Mediterranean. A few miles after its departure from the lake, it has been harnessed for electric power development. The plant was dynamited during the Arab-Israeli war by the Arabs. It lies in a sort of No Man's Land and awaits formal agreement by Transjordan and Israel before it can be put back into operation. Most of the electric power in Israel now is produced expensively by diesel-driven generators.

From the Sea of Galilee, the river flows in a shallow-narrow bed. It is a beautiful stream, the color being a milky green. From some of the white clays comes a deposit which is found even in the Dead Sea, the river carrying it in varying amounts, depending not so much on rains as on the slow release of the deep-placed white clays. There is no more beautiful valley than that called after the river.

Geologists say this valley was formed by the break in the originally connected tablelands of Israel and Transjordan. The climate is warm in winter and hot in summer. Date palms, bananas, tomatoes, and other crops flourish under irrigation. It is a perpetual hothouse, needing no glass-enclosed protection.

The Jordan emerges from the Jordan Valley into the plains of Jericho and Shittim, which lie west and east of the river. Here enter two small streams.

There is even richer vegetation here than in the Jordan Valley, but one comes rapidly to the desolation in which is the oasis of Jericho. The old city is about two miles from the shabby, modern one. A hill strewn with broken bits of pottery is about all that is left of the city whose walls came tumbling down in what is one of the great Biblical stories of God's might.

The Dead Sea has no outlet. It is beautiful on a sunny day. Every day the Jordan pours an estimated seven million tons of chemically rich waters into the vast cauldron of the Dead Sea. There are no shells on its beaches. In its waters there is life, but it is primitive and may be seen chiefly by microscopic investigation. The great heat evaporates the water. A bather cannot sink in it. It is written that Titus, when he had conquered Jerusalem in 90 A.D., carried out a gruesome experiment. He had a number of slaves chained together and flung into the sea. They were natives. They kept their heads and earned their lives by bringing themselves upright and remaining afloat.

There is a chemical smell there. Two potash and chemical plants, interrupted by the Arab war, soon are to resume work.

Here, where the Jordan ends, one may look toward Moab and Nebo and the hill they say was the Mount of Temptation. So small is the country it was easily possible for Moses to see literally all of it from the peaks of Nebo which stand 4,000 feet above the end of the Jordan.

Standing there in the tortured territory about the Dead Sea, one is close to new settlements which the Jews are bravely building. Beyond the sea the desert reaches far on down into the desert region called "The Negeb." It is not true desert, being soil, not sand. It needs only water to bloom. Here, too, are new settlements by the Jews who are determined to build all their new nation.

There exist great plans to water this area—from the Jordan. There are plans to create a TVA of the Jordan Valley—to impound the waters and the floods from melting snows on Mount Hermon and the winter rains. Already there is a six-inch water pipeline into Beersheba. A 20-inch line will open in August. The Jordan, too, will supply electric power from that project of the future.

I made the sentimental journey along the Jordan as close as road could make it. Always I found myself thinking, as I saw the river move from its mountain course to the lakes and beyond to the dead salt sea, of the Old Testament prophets who knew it, and of its association with the Christ and of how many churches rang with hymns of the Jordan. I remembered my own boyhood and a grandmother who would walk out on our farmhouse porch in Tennessee from which we could see the Tennessee River, and say "Son, we all have one more river to cross—the River of Jordan."

It was to me more than a river as I saw it in all its moods. It is not a large river, but I knew no matter where I saw it, there in the lonely hills, in its pastoral reaches of the delta, or in the rush down to the tortured, dismaying deadness about the salt sea that at last receives it, that it was a river which flows through the hearts of many men and women throughout the world. It was never just a river.

18

"The Anemones Red in the Grass"

THE VIA MARIS, Israel—We were on the way to Nazareth and the way led along The Via Maris—the way to the sea—the route that conquerers from the dim edges of recorded history have taken across Palestine and Israel, which historically has been a bridgeway of war since the first recorded movements of men and troops emerged from the mists of antiquity.

The sense of history was so great one could almost feel it. Joe Davis, a young New Zealander who served in the British Army with distinction and later with equal merit in the Israeli war that established a nation, and who knows his new country inch by inch, stopped the car as it rolled into the pass and the beautiful Jesreel Valley opened before us.

On the left was an old hill where archaeologists are digging. Here was Meggido. They have uncovered Solomon's fortress, with its stables for his horses that drew his iron chariots. Across from it is the site of the old town Leggio, corrupted by the Arabs to Lejun, which was called that because the Romans had a legion there guarding the pass in their time. The place of the Legion came to be called Lejun.

Through the pass came the great war lords of the Egyptians, Alexander the Great, Nebuchadnessar with his hordes of men glittering with armor and spears; the Persians, the Crusaders, the Moslems, the British, and, finally, after 2,000 years, the Israeli army once again. There is no road in all the world that has known the tramp of so many armies.

Since the pass was always guarded and defended, there were always great battles there on the plains before it. In an Egyptian temple unearthed years ago were writings describing the battles

fought there by Egyptian King Thothmes in 1478 B. C. The dust
of battle has hung over it since. So often was there war on the
plains the old prophets said that here, on the field of Armageddon, would be fought the last battle of mankind.

I stood there by the road, the anemones red in the grass, the
sun warm upon us, the deep and wonderful smell of apricot and
almond blossoms in the air, and I could see it plainly—the wild
bearded men with the sun on their spears and glinting from their
shields and breastplates, trudging along the wide trail, the sea
behind them, and the mountains in their faces. They marched
there for generations, praying to strange gods, making sacrifices,
leaving their bones there to salt the earth.

It is yet a rich valley.

After them came the Crusaders, fighting there with the Moslems, and winning the pass, to go on and build forts and churches
along the coast. They were to stay more than a 100 years. When
they were driven out, they left behind them children and wives
so that from then on there were Christian Arabs here. They took
with them learning from the Arabs and went back to extinguish
the darkness of the Middle Ages. The richly clad, victorious
Moslems passed that way in triumph. Lord Allenby and his
British appeared in 1916, and, finally, the Iraquians and the
Palestinian Arabs fight on the plains and hills until driven out
by the Israeli army of partisans. One could stand there and see it.

To our left we could see Nazareth, an Arab town high on the
Galilean hill. Straight ahead was Mount Tabor, which is a
symbol of courage and resistance in Jewish history. Standing
there looking at the distant mountain one could picture the
smallness of the times and the armies that fought in the early
days. It was on Tabor the tribes of Israel were gathered together
by Deborah and led to battle against the Canaanites. It was on
Mount Tabor the Insurgent Jews fortified themselves against
the Romans. The ruins of their defenses yet are there.

To the right were the hills of Gilboa. King Saul knew them
well; too well, indeed. It was there, 1,000 years before Christ,
that his army was routed and he fell upon his sword, rather than
be captured. I came back to the hotel later and looked this up
and found David's lamentation over Saul and Jonathan:

"The beauty of Israel is slain upon the high places;
How are the mighty fallen . . .
Ye mountains of Gilboa, let there be no dew,
Neither let there be rain upon you nor fields of offerings,
For there the shield of the mighty is cast away the shield of
Saul . . ."

There they were before us, a chain of hills fading away in the
haze. It almost seemed the air should be heavy, or that a voice
ought to prophesy, a bush burst into flame, or a shaft of light
break through from the heavens. But there was only the silence,
the flowers, the soft wind, a boy herding goats on a slope, and
the faint voices of the many dead crying out from the plain of
Jesreel and the hills that ring here about . . . only that.

So we got back into our car and started it on down the road
into the valley, green and fresh from a recent rain, and finally
the road turned left and we began to climb the Galilean hills
toward Nazareth.

"Here," said Joe Davis, out of the silence, "is where our forces
turned left to come in from behind Nazareth and drove out the
Iraquians and the Palestinian Arab Army. There was heavy
fighting farther on . . ."

Behind us the ancient valley was green and still, heavy with
history and her dead. . . . Armageddon—patiently awaiting the
last battle of all time.

We climbed the hill, seeing the houses blasted by war and
came unto the Arab city of Nazareth. It is not much of a town.
One recalls here the first mention of it in Holy Writ.

When Philip told Nathanael of Jesus, Nathanael said, "Can
anything good come out of Nazareth?"

It was Jesus who gave meaning to this town which clings to
the slopes of a Galilean hill about 400 feet above the Plain of
Jezreel. Jews fled to it after the destruction of the Temple by
the Assyrians. They remained there until the seventh century.
Its present-day inhabitants are believed descended from the Crusaders. Most of them are Arabs and most of them are Christians.
But the town is Arab, dirty and slovenly. There are many
churches, cold and dank. Almost all claim, with no hope of
verification, to be built on some holy spot.

There is one with some claim to authenticity which has at least slight merit. The Greeks have a church built over an old synagogue. It is at the edge of the oldest part of the town. There are ancient foundations there. It is believed this was the synagogue where Jesus preached. I looked it up:

"And He came to Nazareth, where He had been brought up, and, as was His custom, He went into the synagogue on the Sabbath day, and stood up for to read. . . . And they all in the synagogue when they heard these things, were filled with wrath, and rose up, and thrust Him out of the city, and led Him unto the brow of the hill whereon their town was built, that they might cast Him down headlong. But He passed through the midst of them and went His way. . . ."

"Mary's Well" is there. It, too, probably is authentic. The town still uses it. It is walled off with concrete and has iron pipes from which the water flows. Women still come to it for water. Now and then one will see the graceful earthen pitchers such as were used in Biblical days. But, for the most part, the vessel now favored is an old "jerry can" such as the armies used to transport gasoline and water. To see a dirty village Arab slouch in with a dented, rusting jerry can does something to illusions.

They lead a harrassed life, too, do the poor things who come there for water. Tourists are forever trying to photograph them and they, weary of it, are continually trying to thwart the tourists and the cameras.

The Christian Arab guides will not, I think, enter into the gates of Heaven. They have all the vices of the Levant and few of the Christian virtues. When the Israeli army won, the Christian cafe owners hurriedly changed the names of their cafes from those with Arabic names to "Cafe David," "Cafe Israel," and so on.

In one of the shops where I went to purchase a Bible bound with olive wood, I knew enough to look before I bought. I had a hard search before I found a Bible to buy. Most of them were Gideon Bibles stolen from hotels and bound in Arab shops.

The old bazaar section is typically Arab, which is to say it is picturesque because it is dirty, the streets narrow, the Arabs dirty in their robes, and the sewage runs in the middle of the restricted passageways. I think it is principally the dirt which makes for picturesqueness. In other old Arab towns from which the Arabs fled at the outbreak of war and which now are occupied by Jewish immigrants, with sanitation and health measures enforced, the picturesqueness is all gone. I think it must be the dirt and the squalor.

The food in the cafes was good. (One does not look in the kitchen.) There were plates of young fresh onions, radishes and lettuce. The latter I left alone. Dysentery is easy to come by and is a stubborn visitor. But, the bean curd was wonderful. It is scooped up with pieces of Arab bread. We had shishlack, and because it was good, had kebab as well, with potatoes and cooked onions. The smells of the cafe were tremendous and wonderful, being a mixture of the town, of mutton, garlic, onions, peppers, spices, cheese and of broiling lamb. I loved it.

The street scenes in the new town are fabulous. There are donkeys. There are camels. There are rich cars and old ones. There are bars, wine shops, tourist traps and cafes. There are Israeli soldiers. Arabs are there, dirty ones and rich ones, in dirty, cotton robes and in rich, "Effendi" dress. There are Arabs in Western dress. There are the Arab guides with their canes, Levantine and shrewd.

But, one of them, at the door of the old synagogue where Christ may once have preached, said something which reflects the town and the Arabs who stayed and, for that matter, the attitude of many weary, hungry, poor people of regions which have known war for centuries. "We don't care who rules us or who wins," he said, "Arab or Israeli. All we care about is peace." The Arab is a muchly abused person—largely by his own leaders.

It was my second visit to Nazareth. I have never liked it. It is easy to understand why Nathanael was a skeptic. As far as I am concerned nothing good has come out of it, save the cafe food, since Christ left it.

I would like to have seen it in the days when the Tribe of Joseph started on the long walk to Bethlehem. It could not have been more than a small, poor, obscure village in the hills. Certainly it was never important until the birth of Christ. I imagine it was a dirty, slovenly collection of mud and stone houses about the spring, with the poorer persons living out from it with their small herds of goats and sheep. The old records show there once were great forests of oaks on the hills. There are stunted oaks there now. They were reduced by the hooves of goats and sheep and the erosion that followed them. Now, after 20 years of reforestation, they are beginning to grow larger.

We left the town. Along the way were houses destroyed by demolition or shell fire. Below us, in the Jezreel Valley, the shadows were gathering. Ghosts seemed to people it and the red banks of anemones looked like blood in the grass, there where Armageddon waits.

19

Samson, Billy Rose, and Beersheba

Beersheba—I was riding out past Migdal into Samson's country, where the big fellow roamed, ranged and had girl trouble—and I thought that Billy Rose, who has pulled down a few temples of pretense and slain a few Philistines himself, would get a thrill out of the fact the car in which I was riding was called "The Billy Rose Car."

There is a twin to it. When Showman and Columnist Billy Rose was in Israel two years ago he saw the pitifully few cars the boys in the Information Office had in their stables. When he returned home he and a friend shipped over two four-door touring cars. All I can say to the friend is he should be in show business, write a column and have Eleanor Holm for a wife. I say this because the cars are called "The Billy Rose Cars." The boys look after them as if they were a maharajah's plated Rolls-Royces. I never met a gift, outside food for a starving man, more appreciated or used than this one.

Samson's country is pleasant. There are rolling hills of grass and grain. It was somewhere near here he slew the lion and the Philistines. His wife was from near-by Ascalon. It was after she betrayed his secret he tied the tails of foxes together, fired them and turned them loose in the fields of Philistine corn. During the recent war with the Arabs the Israeli army had a commando unit operating in this territory. They called themselves "Samson's Foxes" and went about happily blowing up Arab installations and otherwise harrying the modern-day Philistines.

The Israelis used some of the Biblical phrases in the war. It was "Operation Ten Plagues" which enabled them to fan out beyond the Egyptian army and pin them in the Faluja pocket, from which the hungry and sick men were evacuated after the armistice. So, in the twentieth century the Children of Israel visited plagues upon the unhappy Egyptians in the form of two by-passing columns which won for Israel the long strip of coast she now holds.

We went into the old British police station which was held at the northern corner of the pocket. It is at a place called Iraq Suwedian. We had a look at it. It overlooks the plains in both directions. It is an abandoned shambles, filled with shell holes. In two rooms there are great splashes of blood upon the wall and onto the ceiling where some poor devil of an Egyptian died for King Farouk.

Ascalon was a center of Philistine culture and a fortress against ancient Israel. The old town existed into the middle ages. It is now a mound of ruins.

When King Saul was killed by the Philistines on distant Mount Gilboa, David mourned him, saying, "Publish it not in the streets of Ascalon, lest the daughters of the Philistines rejoice. . . ."

We went on, seeing the workers digging the trench for the 20-inch pipe line to bring water to Beersheba, which exists from wells and a six-inch line already there. Behind the machines and men digging the trench were others lowering the big sections of pipe to pipe-fitters who joined it up.

It is lonely country, and arid, but water will change it. The traffic of truck-laden pipes was heavy but at last I saw the graceful minaret of the principal mosque at Beersheba—the first sign of the ancient town one sees. It has changed.

Here now, is a rootin', tootin' wild West frontier town where they talk Hebrew and ride both camels and jeeps.

This ancient town of Abraham and Jacob is the hopping-off place for the desert—the Negeb—where the Israelis are pushing their water line and where some 20 farm settlements are wrestling with conditions that are tough as anything our own West knew, with the Arab war as substitute for our Indian wars.

It is a frontier town complete to the barrooms (where no one gets drunk). The soldiers, pipeline workers and builders wear beards and pistols. It is frontier in appearance and reality as to people, cafes and hotels. But it differs in that there is no drunkenness and there are no painted ladies and no gambling joints.

Israel still is a dedicated country. But it is dusty, war-torn and primitive. Big trucks go rumbling through with their loads of pipe and machinery. Farm trucks come in for supplies. Farmers and workers have soft drinks, beer or some of the sweet Carmel wine at one of the small, raw-new cafes. They are not a getting-drunk people. Their kids come into the cafes, all of which are labeled bars as well, and have the old European "soda"—raspberry flavor and soda water.

Dusty, robed, bearded Bedouins and their camels come to town. They don't bother about and are not surprised at the change. The Bedouins were there when recorded history dawned. They are still there in the Negeb, their flocks of camels, goats and donkeys on the hills, herded by small, robed boys, and their black hair-tents are pitched on the slopes hard by some oasis, well or spring. They have the philosophy of the desert, that nothing save food and water is really important.

It is a wild West town, too, because of the cattle rustlers and smugglers. One of Israel's toughest problems is cattle and horse stealing. Arabs come over the borders at night to raid the small settlements of stock. In the Negeb the great smuggling business is hashish. Police showed us some of their captures. Hashish is narcotic weed. When dried and ground, the result can be pressed into a cake. It looks like a cake of hardened snuff and it smells like dried hay. But it sells for $15 a pound. Bedouins run it through the desert to Egypt. It comes through from Syria and Lebanon. Most of it is produced in Turkey and Syria. The Bedouins travel by night, holing up with their camels in some deep ravine by day. It is almost impossible to catch them.

Egypt takes most of the supply. It is the poor man's dream powder and it testifies to the misery of the poor in Egypt. The drug has corrupted the Egyptian police, which do not try to capture the smugglers. At least, some of the police work with the smugglers.

Stock stealing by Arabs attained such proportions the cattle on all border farms are brought at night to a single corral, or stabled, with guards. Some of the hashish smugglers are caught, but most of them get through, traveling at night and hiding by day in the great unoccupied stretches of the Negeb.

I saw Beersheba last in 1946. It was then a dusty, sleepy, quiet
Arab town to which tourists came to see the picturesqueness and
to watch the primitive use of Abraham's wells, seven of them,
where old water chains, turned by donkeys or camels, pull up
the water in pitch-coated wooden cups, each holding about a
quart. The streets were quiet. The shops were shabbily "quaint."
There were just two streets, with Arab mud huts clustered about
the edges of the town. Eucalyptus and tamarisk trees made the
town pleasant. I remembered the first sign of the town one saw
was the minaret of the mosque sending its slender tower up above
the rise of ground which obscured the town itself.

On this revisit, I was agape at the changes. As our car sped
up the hill and the town opened before us, to the left was a
brand-new village of small, modern one-and-a-half-room houses,
plus bathroom. The sound of explosions came to us. Later I
learned that soldiers were detecting and detonating land mines
left from "the war" on a piece of ground where new building
was to begin. (It is not yet safe to walk around the battlefields
of the recent war. Almost every week someone gets hurt with
mines or detonators despite a police and press campaign of warn-
ing. Six young boys were killed recently by one mine, which they
found and set off by tossing a rock on it.)

I saw that old Beersheba (not so old really, since the "modern"
buildings were built in 1900) was no more. Dust rose continually
from it. Traffic bustled through it. The sweating, muscled laborers toiled with heavy loads; soldiers came and went; pistol-
wearing guards and MPs were about. Only the Bedouins slouched
along, seemingly unimpressed.

Many of the buildings, mostly one-story, were war wrecked.
They are being restored into small shops. The chief one of Beersheba's Biblical wells, the one closest in town, is now behind a
new gasoline pump and station, the sign of which is riddled with
bullet holes. It was in the line of fire in some of the street fighting
between Israeli and Arab troops.

The well dates back to the time of the old patriarch whose
flocks grazed in the arid lands about Beersheba. Abraham likely
was a Bedouin, certainly he was a shepherd patriarch. It was
at this Beersheba Abraham made his covenant with Abimelech.

Out of dusty, frontier-town Beersheba, the old military road leads straight into the Negeb, which in Hebrew means "dry." It is dry, but it is not true desert, although it is so called. The soil needs only water.

The road runs, too, to heroism and sacrifice.

Along the way were the Bedouins, their tents along the slopes, their flocks grazing the short, tough grass which grows the year around in small clumps. Here and there were large flocks of camels. Now and then we passed a Bedouin plowing with a camel, his plow little different from the primitive type used for hundreds of years. The Bedouin so employed is, of course, an obsolete economic unit. He and his camel can live meagerly in the desert. He plows where he wishes, to raise a few vegetables and a little wheat. The old Moslem law allowed a man to harvest a crop where he was allowed to plow. The law still holds. The Bedouins early made a treaty with Israel which allows them their ancient rights. But roads and water are coming, as are trucks and jeeps. The Arab with the camel is almost as obsolete economically as the Southern farmer with one mule.

During the Winter, and as late as mid-April, sudden floods sweep through the dry country from the rains of the Hebron mountains. They surge mightily through otherwise dry water courses, cutting huge areas out of the hills and creating vast eroded territories. In their wake the grasses spring up, the flowers bloom in profusion, anemones, purple sage and a clover new to me, the blossom of which was blue and smelled of honey. There was also a yellow flower which looked like mustard, but was not. Once we saw a stork, lone and large, picking away at something in the grass. The stork and many other birds, unseen in Israel in many years, are coming back with the planting of crops and trees.

Along part of the way was the bed of the old Turkish railway which ran to Egypt. The Turks were here for hundreds of years and the country suffers yet from that harsh, ruthless occupation. As late as 1916 the Turks issued an almost unbelievable decree ordering every tree in the country cut down. There were not many left, even then, so wastefully had the trees been cut through the centuries. But, with the war on and the British invading, the Turks needed wood to run their trains and to build fortifications. To possess a tree was a crime. So it is today that save for one or two isolated regions all the trees one sees in Israel and Jordan Palestine are not more than 30 years old. Hundreds of men work daily over Jerusalem planting trees, chiefly eucalyptus, tamarack, cypress and, of course, fruit trees, apricot, date, fig, orange, plum and olive.

We were on our way to the southernmost Jewish farm settlement, called Revivim. The word means dew, and it was given this settlement because near it were a curious assortment of small hills, each terraced so well the work had lasted for hundreds of years since the last hand worked there. Scientists figured out that they were so arranged that silken cloths erected there would catch the heavy dewfall and drain it off to the slopes. In the Negeb there are ruins of the old cities which once supported populations of 20,000 and more in the days of the Byzantine Empire when the ancient trade routes led through the desert. When the empire and trade died they perished, too. But once they were there and once they lived. Their ruins do not tell how.

In the days of the mandate the Jewish program was to set out settlements so as to have a claim to land and so as to provide defense outposts when, and if, it came to a fight. They proved themselves both ways—as producers of food and outposts.

This one was set down 25 miles south of the last city, Beersheba, beside a small spring which was salty, but possible to drink. That was 1943.

Along the way we passed ruins, those of the Turks, and more recent ones of British outposts. But we soon came on the uglier ones, sand-bagged and walled in . . . Egyptian gun positions of two and three years ago. They commanded the road along which we drove.

At Revivim it was like a fort. They had driven off many Egyptian raids. The settlement, established in 1943, had also fought the desert well. They had built catch basins for the flood. For about five hours millions of tons of water roared through the dry course, tearing and sweeping all before it on its way to the sea. A few hours later the course was bone dry again. I doubt if any people anywhere have ever worked so hard or so desperately as these young men and women.

Their buildings were fenced about with barbed wire. There were trenches and machinegun positions at each corner. Some of their buildings had been demolished. For weeks they had lived in a large cave, which also served as a hospital for troops thereabout. The cave is an old one of the Byzantine caravan days and undoubtedly was a caravansary of those times.

By painful trial-and-error method they had learned that olive trees, dates and figs would do well if given a little water from time to time. They found, too, the Negeb soil would grow almost any vegetable known. The settlement already is famous for its tomatoes and beans. From their catch basins they irrigate their large vegetable fields.

Of the original settlers 20 are left. Those that married and had babies were sent elsewhere. It was not then a place for babies. It soon will be. A nursery house is going up.

They have now a piece of land near Beersheba where the water line comes where they grow feed for cattle. On the day we arrived they were just feeding the 20 cows—Holsteins—sent them the day before in a shipment arrived from America and paid for by friends in that country.

Their lives are lonely ones, without movies or recreation, yet they are but a few of the many hundreds who so volunteered to help build a country. Most of these were "Sabras," the native born, and none spoke English. Soon, they said, all traces of war would be gone. But it was like one of our old settlements in America—with trenches and machinegun posts instead of block-houses and log walls. This country was not won easily. And the hardest job—the economic one—is ahead.

20

The Work of Soil, Sun and Diet

W<small>E PULLED OUT</small> of Revivim, the sun glinting on its impounded waters so arduously caught and yet auguring much for the future. There is enough water loosed from the mountain rains and floods to recreate the desert if man's ingenuity can catch it.

In a small corral four young girls, about 18, in work-stained overalls, were laughing and shouting as they fed young Holstein calves, part of a small herd of cattle which had arrived the day before after a long journey from the United States where funds had been gathered to purchase the cows. Further south was the army.

In my mind was the phrase, "Dan to Beersheba." I had seen the people at work above Dan and below Beersheba and in between.

They were just people, as they are anywhere else, with more complexities confronting them because of history and the war and the agonies leading to, and through, the agony of a nation's birth.

They are a people in transition, and the ferment of it is great. Old cultures, and old attitudes jar one another. These are attitudes ranging from the nihilists of Russia, who quite understandably thought any government was bad since all they had known was the Tsars and the anti-Zionist Soviets, to many theories of government. There are neuroses brought from many lands.

All these move toward a common culture which is locked in the books of the future.

I cannot bring into focus all the vast complexities of this tremendous experience and vitality called Israel . . . the newest state, and the oldest . . . the one which is not at all static, but which is constantly expanding with a vast variety of peoples, tongues and backgrounds. This is being done in a world political situation which is really that of a little cold war within a large, world-wide cold war.

The cost of it is great. The problems of it are enormous. In the past, no country has been built without a semiexploitation period. Here there is the effort to build a country and maintain social services such as insurance, wage and hour laws, and public health.

Here is a small country bringing in immigrants at a furious rate. Many of them, the older ones, will never be truly absorbed. They will supply an unskilled labor force protected by a minimum wage which presently is equivalent to about 65 cents an hour. They can be used only as fast as the work is available. The work is available only as fast as building materials are at hand, and when industry expands.

Meanwhile, the painful condition of the immigrant camps must be endured, and the slow progress of integrating the new-comers into the economy must be tugged at and worried with inadequately—because of the reasons aforesaid. A new nation cannot stand alone as soon as it is born. This one faces problems which are radically different from that of other nations, but also has all the usual ones.

The variety of the people who come is amazing, fascinating and constitutes a new chapter in history. It is something new under the sun. The North Africans, particularly the Moroccans, and the Iraquians, offer the most difficulty in assimilation.

For centuries their background, or environment, has been that of an Arabic people. They have lived in the crowded quarters and alleyways of more or less isolated states. Their outlook, even their appearance, is that of their Arab neighbors. They have never been allowed land, therefore they know nothing of it. They have lived hard, desperate lives in which acute poverty demanded they be sly, cunning and shrewd. It is not easy to bring such people into the sun, so to speak, and to plant them on the land.

The problem becomes twofold. It is both economic and social. The best-planned budgets become meaningless when Iraq informs Israel that about 70,000, possibly 150,000, persons wish to come to Israel. The housing plans, the food allotments—all these go out the window. Egypt and other Arab states arm. Israel must do the same. That is the huge economic meaning of it. The social task is almost as large.

All this makes of Israel many things. It makes it among others, a giant test tube in human and sociological observation. One thing is clear. I saw a little of it in 1946. I recall writing then of the healthy-looking children, large and blooming, who could hardly be believed to be the children of their small, often stunted, fathers and mothers. It was possible then to see what environment, fresh air, sun, orange juice, milk, bread, eggs and meat would do. All this was shaping their faces and their bodies as corn and environment shaped the faces of the Europeans who came to settle and conquer America.

Now I have seen it in even more dramatic form. Children who came here in ages from infancy up to 10 and 12 years are changing so fast one may almost see it. They arrived looking more or less like their parents, the Yemenites, the Moroccans, the Tripolitanians—furtive, suspicious, dirty, often without any concept of what the new country was. They expected it to be, perhaps, a bed of roses and ease. Their parents, largely illiterate, did not know it to be a nation which works hard and which must work even harder. Most of these have not changed and will not, save in minor ways.

But their children! It is fantastic. They bloom and they grow. They put on weight. Their faces are bright. I have seen them settled on the land and still in immigrant camps; in kindergarten learning Hebrew and new songs—and they are amazing. I do not know how much environment can do—but I have seen that it can work miracles.

They will never be like their parents. They will never wail at the wall or grow symbolic curls or wear costumes dating back to the days of the destruction of the temple. They are growing in the sun and in the light of freedom and knowledge.

Climate, diet, sun and soil are at work and already they are producing a biological change, a new physical type.

The "Sabra," as those born in Palestine, and now Israel, are called, after the tough, native cactus plant, is of course a highly nationalistic person. Our own history illustrates well that sort of attitude. In the early years of the Republic the nationalism was extreme and for generations our July 4th celebrations consisted almost entirely of eagle screams.

The concentration on Hebrew as a language and on a study of ancient Hebrew history has been called egocentric and "cultural claustrophobia." In a sense it is both. But, it is an inevitable part of the development of a new nation and a common language of its own is a powerful incentive. People still pour into the land. The ferment will be a long time in producing its final product—the national culture and the Israeli who will illustrate it by his life, his arts, his literature and his politics.

Those who have had an opportunity to see and feel the heart-beat and the spirit of all that is bound up in the word "Israel" know its strength and its potential for higher standards of human values in a land long lost in feudal decay.

There are in it the voices of the old prophets, the mournings and ancient sorrowings of thousands in countless corners of the world from the time of Cyrus, and of Titus. There are in it the tears and agonies of the millions who suffered and died under Hitler. To create it bricks were made without straw and men and women made it a dream worth dying for. I cannot help but believe they will make it something worth living for.